Freewheeling

Bicycling the Open Road

Freewheeling

Bicycling the Open Road

Gary Ferguson

ILLUSTRATIONS BY BETSY JAMES

The Mountaineers • Seattle

THE MOUNTAINEERS: Organized 1906
"...to encourage a spirit of good fellowship
among all lovers of outdoor life."

© Gary Ferguson 1984
All rights reserved
Published by The Mountaineers
306 2nd Ave. West, Seattle, Washington 98119
Published simultaneously in Canada by Douglas & McIntyre, Ltd.
1615 Venables St., Vancouver, British Columbia V5L 2H1
Manufactured in the United States of America
Edited by Ann Cleeland
Cover design by Marge Mueller
Book design by Barbara Haner
09 8 7 6
5 4 3 2

Library of Congress Cataloging in Publication Data
Ferguson, Gary, 1956-
      Freewheeling: bicycling the open road.

      Bibliography: p.
      Includes index.
      1. Bicycle touring. I. Title.
GV1044.F47   1984   796.6   84-16643
ISBN 0-89886-047-4

To Dad, who always went the distance...

Contents

Introduction

Despite the many pleasures of a long-distance cycling trip, there can be some definite pains about the whole affair (besides those that settle in your backside). There are wind and rain and heat to contend with, as well as the psychological hurdle of being reduced to little more than "slow moving traffic, keeping right."

But we pedal bravely on, balanced precariously on that thin white line — past dogs, dust, and dented rims, past gravel, grit, and grumbling motorists. And, should cycle and cyclist arrive at the far end of a one-way trip in one piece, it's not uncommon to break out in a cold sweat as our faithful companion is carted off to the bowels of an airplane or bus, to undoubtedly be buried beneath two tons of shifting luggage.

But from either speculation or experience, you're probably convinced that the good aspects of distance riding outweigh the bad. It's hard to beat the exhilarating feeling of pedaling through the brisk morning air, the people encountered along the way, the slow, deliberate discovery of an exciting new nook or cranny of the world. Seventy-five miles of pumping pedals tends to make one appreciate the simple comforts: how fantastic food tastes, how soothing a shower can be, how good the ground feels to fall asleep on.

Indeed, the joys of long-distance cycling need no further introduction. They will turn into fond memories without help from anyone. This book, then, will show you how to keep up the pleasures by putting a lid on the pains. At first, some of the bits of advice offered between these covers may seem a bit painful in themselves: learning a few essential repairs, researching your proposed route, designing a bicycling budget. But believe me, these pains are infinitely more tolerable than their alternatives. Perhaps more than most forms of recreation, long-distance cycling requires some thoughtful preparation if it is to be enjoyed to its fullest.

Don't get me wrong. The last thing I want to do is turn you into an "elitist" when it comes to taking 10-speed trips. My first 100-mile day trip was with one friend, at age 14. He had a three-speed English Racer, and I had a five-speed Sting-Ray. I eventually advanced to overnighters by tying a giant sleeping bag wrapped in plastic to a flimsy carrier. It was a heck of a lot of fun. But over the long haul—when you plan to be on the road for several days or even weeks and will be covering several hundred miles—the time available for enjoyable, carefree riding will be directly proportional to your fitness, equipment, and ability to respond to the problems that will undoubtedly occur along the way.

I sincerely hope that all of your flats will be front ones, that the Texas wind will have mercy on you, and that all RV drivers will choose vacation routes different from yours.

1

Heading for the Hills

It's true. No other form of travel can hand you the world in such rich and varied form. Only the long-distance cyclist moves fast enough to experience a patchwork of landscapes and cultures, yet slow enough to glimpse their connecting threads. Indeed, such a vacation is not so much a happening, as an unfolding. Years from now, you may be surprised to discover that when you sit back and think about all your past treks and travels, the ones taken by bicycle seem to be among the first to surface. Those memories are always strange, wonderful mixes of quiet and noise, forest and concrete, sun and rain, hills crawling up and hills screaming down. And they're usually all that's needed to ignite an itch in you to once again straddle that saddle and head for the hills.

It may surprise you to learn that there are many different ways in which to tour by bike—by yourself or in a group, with sag wagons or fully self-contained, one to a bike or a bike built for two. Each is so very different from the others that it's almost like trying another sport entirely. In the following pages we'll take a close look at these riding options and just what makes each of them worth your careful consideration.

GOING ALONE

As is true with virtually any form of travel, going it alone offers a rather mixed bag of blessings. On the negative side, if you plan on camping out you will have to carry all the equipment yourself. Things like

tools, tents, and food, which are often shared within a group, all end up in your bags. (Forget the souvenirs!) After a tough day on the road, there will be no one to help set up camp or get dinner going, no one to help dry things out and repack after a rain. You will have to be the expert for all repairs that may be needed, and you will have to carry the appropriate spare parts. On those long, boring afternoons that almost always occur on an extended tour, there will be no one around to help break the monotony. And when the headwinds blow, one of the most effective defenses the cyclist can have—drafting behind a partner—simply won't be an option that's open to you.

On the plus side, you'll have absolute freedom to go where you want, when you want to. If you like to sleep late and ride in the afternoons, there will be no one around to suggest you do otherwise. If you feel like a million bucks and decide to go for a 125-mile day, there will be no need to consider anyone else's abilities. And, speaking of abilities, the single biggest advantage of solo travel is that you can always ride at the cadence that is right for you; there's no stopping and waiting for slower companions and, likewise, no rush to hurry and catch up with an impatient leader. The road, and the world it leads to, is all yours.

If you do decide to camp with your bicycle alone, it's a very good idea to take a couple of short "shakedown" overnighters to make sure that you're comfortable with the load level and general operations. You may, for instance, find that you'll have to add a set of front panniers to your outfit to handle all the equipment. This is going to pinch your pocketbook a bit, as well as add a significant amount of weight and wind drag. Even if it seems like you can keep your equipment confined to rear panniers and a front bag, is there enough room to stuff in a few groceries late in the day for the evening meal?

You can make substantial cuts in space and weight without sacrificing comfort by choosing your equipment carefully. Instead of a tent, for instance, you may elect to camp with a bivy sack. These are certainly much more confining than a good backpacking tent, but can be had for less money, less room, and less weight. Instead of taking a full-length foam pad, use one that extends only from your shoulders to just past your hips. You may want to consider using a down sleeping bag, since it will stuff into a slightly smaller size than will a synthetic bag. Take fewer clothes, especially if laundromats will be plentiful along your route, and in cool weather, opt for the new lightweight synthetics that offer good insulation with minimum thickness.

Of course, if the budget allows, a great way to reduce your load is to plan to stay in motels and eat meals out. You'll be amazed at the additional freedom that this allows, and it may be an especially good way to go at those times when you don't feel that you're in good enough shape to carry an additional 35 to 40 pounds up steep grades.

Because there are no opportunities for solo riders to break headwinds with a partner, it's very important to make a careful check of the prevailing wind direction along your proposed route (see Chapter 8). If they don't seem favorable, then alter your plans accordingly.

There are, unfortunately, also a few matters of personal safety that people who travel alone should consider. This discussion isn't meant to discourage prospective solo cyclists. Indeed, the more of the world you can see from the saddle, the better. It does pay, however, to understand the uncomfortable situations that do exist in various places and then make an effort to plan your activities around them.

Though far from fair, it seems that the lone woman is often left to bear the biggest brunt of uncomfortable situations—most of them harmless, yet certainly unnerving. More often than not, the source of the problem is usually a man or group of men who feels it necessary to inflate their flat senses of virility with indiscriminate blasts of hot air. Though it's very rare that these idiotic displays ever go past the verbal stage, it nevertheless doesn't hurt to keep yourself isolated from the areas where paper tigers seem proudest of their stripes.

The best way for single women to steer clear of troublesome situations is to keep as low a profile as possible. Don't make it a common topic of conversation that you're traveling alone. Many groups split up during the day and reunite in the evening, so using such a story line should not be met with skepticism. Some women, if riding late in the evening, will don clothes and a helmet that tend to make them fairly indistinguishable from a man. Revealing attire such as halter tops will do little but invite unwanted comments, and in many European countries, any kind of "American" clothing is just what many Romeos keep their eyes open for. In parts of Mexico, shorts are usually reserved for "ladies of the evening."

And, speaking of foreign countries, you would do well to remember that in some places—especially the Middle East—your 10-speed declaration of independence will not be viewed with admiration by most of society. It is not unimaginable that you'll one day find yourself at the blunt end of some rather scathing remarks by local men. It is best to be patient with and courteous to all such affronts. Here, like everywhere, you will meet some fantastic people. Try to remember that the ones who cannot accept you as you are have thousands of years of strict tradition underlying their attitudes toward what is right and wrong. As is true everywhere, any change in that heritage, whether for good or bad, is never easily accepted.

It's an excellent idea to call or visit the American embassy in such countries before beginning any extensive solo bicycle tour. The personnel there can tell you all about what is considered acceptable behavior and what is not. This is not to tell you to swallow your own beliefs; rather, keep your frustration in check long enough to try to gain a better understanding of why a culture walks in the shoes that it does.

When it comes time to bed down for the night in uncomfortable surroundings, you may prefer to opt for hotels or hostels. Though it's much more adventurous to find little backstreet inns on your own, in large cities both men and women should first ask local authorities about sections of town that have particularly notorious reputations. In many foreign countries there are all-women hotels. You can get their addresses by contacting the appropriate tourist bureau.

If you prefer to sleep outside, sticking to campgrounds along major bike routes will provide you with the welcome company of other cyclists. In areas where no safe facilities are available, just make a call to the local police station. You'll receive a great deal of help if you explain that you are simply looking for a safe place to roll out your bag. (Indeed, this practice will probably turn you into one of the most protected citizens in the country.)

Both men and women soloists should stay clear of places that make good hangouts. Keep away from the American subway and foreign Metro train stations at night, as well as the red light and waterfront shipping districts. Though it's extremely unlikely you'll ever have to use it, learn the word for "help" in all appropriate languages. A whistle is also very effective.

CYCLING WITH OTHERS

No doubt there can also be a fair collection of pluses and problems when you decide to tour with other people. Of course there are the pragmatic bonuses to consider, such as reduced individual weight loads and draft lines to break the wind. But in addition, you'll be seeing so many new things, feeling so many new feelings on an extended tour, that it's just plain terrific to have someone to share them with. As is true with many forms of self-propelled travel, you'll get to know your companions in a way that just doesn't jell when you're watching television together. Going through the challenges of a long ride with someone helps to form a bond of friendship that you may not have thought it possible to achieve.

While differences of opinion and "bad moods" will undoubtedly occur, everyone should feel that he can communicate freely with the other group members. This is often best done over the morning or evening meal, since dispositions are often not suitable for pow-wows during a tough day's ride.

Perhaps the greatest problems occur in groups when a member or members try to impose their pace on someone else. It seems almost a necessity that you first go on a couple of day-trips with all prospective riders to determine "cadence compatibility" and then discuss what each person expects out of the tour with regard to daily mileages, layovers, and the like. This way, there will be far fewer surprises. If there are great differences in abilities, each person should ride at the speed he prefers, and the group may still be able to reunite at the end of the day. If you're lucky enough to have at least two slower and two faster people, some sharing of equipment can still take place. But remember that anytime riders are traveling by themselves, each will need a complete set of tools and spare parts, and have the ability to use them. Finally, keep in mind that there are two sides to the cadence coin: Slowing down your pace to match someone else's can ultimately be as wearing on you as it would be on them to speed up to match yours.

Make a sincere effort to share the responsibilities of a cycling tour—everything from the initial planning of routes and itineraries (if there are to be any) to setting up camp and cooking. Some people prefer

to assign "road duties" before they leave. If someone isn't doing his fair share, discuss it *with him*, rather than behind his back.

On layover days, many groups will split up so that each person can "do his own thing." There is little doubt that this practice leaves everyone a bit more enthusiastic about hitting the road together the next morning.

ORGANIZED TOURS

Organized tours can be a great way to introduce yourself to the world of long-distance cycling. With many tours, you don't even need to own a bike or equipment—it's all provided for you. You'll more than likely be able to glean a good deal of information about the area you're traveling through from leaders of the ride. And, it's quite possible that you'll meet other participants who may turn into perfect partners for future trips.

The secret to having a good experience on a group tour is to do your homework. First of all, form a profile of what you consider to be the "ultimate" group program *for you*. Following are some questions that you'll want to make sure you have answers for.

1. Do you want to take your own bike and equipment, or will you be satisfied with renting?

2. Would you prefer to camp out or stay in hotels or hostels?

3. Does camp cooking suit you, or would you prefer restaurant fare? If camp cooking is agreeable, would you mind sharing in the cooking and cleanup responsibilities?

4. Would you mind carrying your equipment, or do you prefer the freedom that comes from throwing it into a "sag wagon"? (This is a vehicle that carries equipment, and on occasion, gives rides to participants too pooped to pedal.)

5. Can you do your own repairs, or will you need to depend on someone for assistance?

6. How many miles a day would you feel comfortable traveling and over what kind of terrain?

7. Are you primarily interested in riding all day, or would you prefer that an equal amount of time be spent seeing the sights?

Once you complete this picture of what you want, the next step is to contact any of the hundreds of tour companies currently operating in this country and around the world. (A particularly good place to find listings of these is in the commercial and classified ads of bicycling and outdoor magazines.) Once you find one that seems to fit your profile, it's time to whip out a second set of questions—ones aimed not at you, but at the company you're considering riding with:

1. What kind of equipment do they have (if you're planning on renting)? Can they guarantee the proper size bike? (When renting, it's a very good idea to bring your own saddle if you've got one that's well broken in.)

2. What are the qualifications of the leaders? How many will there be per number of people?

3. How big a group is it? Will you be required to ride in one large mass? (Run from these like the plague.)

4. What are the policies regarding refunds if you cancel or get sick?

5. Does the company have insurance covering accidents or injuries? If not, will your own medical insurance cover you?

Like any large assemblage of people, a touring group has a certain personality about it. There will often need to be some give and take on your part to make the program run smoothly. Be flexible. Accept the fact that it may not work out for you to visit every location on the original itinerary. Weather, and even changes requested by the majority of the group members, mean that nothing on an organized tour is absolute. Sign up for a group tour to get a better feeling for distance riding and to meet other people who have, or are gaining, a deep appreciation for the comradery of the open road.

TANDEM TOURING

Touring long distances by tandem can be a rather difficult, though certainly not impossible, undertaking. First, you must realize that to get a tandem that will have the response and feel of a conventional 10-speed, you are going to have to spend a great deal of money (usually *well* over $1,000). The less expensive models will work fine for touring on flat ground with little headwind, but to coax them up any kind of steep grade will take a couple of fullbacks on the saddles.

Also, keep in mind that parts for tandems can be extremely difficult to find on the road. Make sure you know your bike well, and take every possible precaution to equip yourself with any parts that could break down during a trip.

If you do decide that tandem touring is for you, you'll probably have to resign yourself to staying in motels or hostels while on the road. Because there is essentially no more room for loading equipment on a tandem than there is on a regular bike, it's extremely difficult to take adequate provisions for two people to camp out along the way in comfort. Before leaving on any kind of trip that will take you over unfamiliar terrain, practice, practice, practice! Not only do tandems require two people with similar riding capabilities, but they handle very differently from a conventional bicycle. Maneuvering them safely down a steep, curvy road takes an experienced hand at the helm.

On the whole, you should be very dedicated to the concept of tandem touring before you take one on a major ride. A tandem can be a fast, fun machine that allows two people to experience the open road like no other type of bicycling can. If it suits your fancy, your pocketbook, and your mechanical abilities, roll up your sleeves and dig in.

A FINAL WORD

Throughout these pages you will see references made to boredom, frustration, and various other emotional concerns. These are a very real part of a long-distance bicycling tour. By anticipating that such developments may arise, you can also plan what to do about them. As mentioned earlier, if you're traveling in a group it's very important that everyone feels that he can communicate such things to the other members. As long as you've got the proper tools and spare parts available, don't be afraid to ask if you can drop back from the group for a day if that's what you need to work yourself out of your mental rut.

Alternatively, if you're alone when emotional problems hit, it's often a good idea to get away from the road completely for a day or so. Go to a beach, park, or sporting event where there will be ample opportunity to talk with other people. When evening hits, find a busy campground or hostel where you can make some acquaintances of kindred spirits. The fact is that being alone on the road for many days can leave you with a substantial need for other stimuli. By recognizing this need and moving to fulfill it, you'll only add to the good memories of your tour.

Families touring with children may have to deal with emotional problems on a fairly regular basis. As is true for people riding alone, most kids can be brought out of a slump by simply being given a change of pace from the road. Plan something really special for one or two nights a week. Perhaps it will be a motel room with color television, an amusement park, or a zoo. It also helps to plan your road lunches or snacks at unique locations, such as a lake or state park. By plugging "specialties" into your trip on a regular basis, you'll find that children's (as well as adults') tolerance for long days along the white line will be substantially increased.

Essentially, you can expect to feel very intensified versions of the same ups and downs that run through our everyday lives. One of the great things about long-distance touring, however, is that each new stretch of roadway holds the promise of new and exciting people and places. Invariably, just when you begin to wonder if you can push yourself through another day, something happens to profoundly change your outlook. It happens so often on a bike because you tend to move slowly across the land, with plenty of opportunity to stop, look, and listen to the parts of the world that up until now were merely blurs in the rear-view mirror. It may be difficult at first to stop and visit an out-of-the-way place or take the time to see some special event. We are an "on schedule" society. But as a cyclist, you must resign yourself to the fact that you will be operating in a different time frame. Slow down, and drink in as much as you can of what the road has to offer.

2

Bike Works

Unfortunately, there is no one right bike for long-distance travel. If you ask 10 different people which is "best," you'll be lucky if you get fewer than 10 different answers. There are, however, some generally agreed-upon principles that you can use in the selection of a touring bike or in the upgrading of the bike you currently own.

Unless you're very wealthy, the machine that you end up with is going to be a mixture of compromises. The whole objective is to make sure that none of those compromises comes in an area that will severely affect the stability and comfort of the machine. If you're like most riders, you'll probably find that your money is best spent first in the areas of quality frame and wheel construction. If these items are inferior, no amount of upgrading later is going to make the machine a pleasure to ride.

A final word before jumping into these nitty-gritty particulars of the touring machine. It's not such a good idea to load up and take off on a major ride the day after you write the check for your dream machine. Even if you're quite familiar with similar bikes, each will have a little different ride, saddle feel, braking capacity, and center of balance. If at all possible, give yourself a couple of hundred miles of "bare-biking" before trying a major expedition. Let the kinks—both yours as well as the bike's—come to the surface somewhere near the comforts of home.

THE FRAME

Style

There are basically two types of frame styles open to consideration by the serious tourist: the standard "diamond" and the "mixte," a rather

STANDARD DIAMOND FRAME

MIXTE FRAME

updated version of the "woman's" frame left over from the days of the dinosaurs. It's possible for everyone but those cyclists requiring extremely small frame sizes (20 inches or less) to ride an efficiently constructed diamond frame. And they should do so. The diamond is a careful blending of geometry that is currently the strongest, most responsive type of construction available. Because of qualities inherent to their design, mixtes are weaker and tend to have excess "softness" to their ride. This means that instead of the power going into propelling the bike, much of it is instead absorbed by the motion of the frame.

If, however, you require a frame in the 20-inch or under size, a mixte is probably worth your consideration. The diamond-style frame tends to end up with too much "reach" or length in such small sizes, which can also result in a loss of efficient power transfer. While some dealers might suggest that you solve the problem by getting a diamond frame with 26-inch wheels instead of the standard 27-inch, this solution seems appropriate only if you plan to tour in rough country. The additional work involved to travel the same distance on 26-inch wheels, coupled with the fact that there is a shortage of high quality 26-inch rims in much of the world would, for the shorter person, make a mixte with standard wheel size the preferred choice.

Materials

It is at this point that, if not careful, you can enter a world of picky preferences that are totally irrelevant to all but those cycling regularly with the snob set. Generally speaking, most touring bikes that will be under your consideration will be constructed of some sort of steel alloy tubing. It is largely the variations in those alloys that can cause this relatively simple heart of a touring bicycle to soar to well over $2,000.

In order of quality and expense, the most common additives that are combined with steel to produce a satisfactory alloy for bicycles are: carbon, chrome-molybdenum, and molybdenum-manganese. The reason for going to all this trouble and expense with what may seem like exotic materials is that the end result is a metal tube that is thin (and hence weighs less), yet has a high degree of strength and resilience. It is this latter quality—a sort of tight springiness—that you will probably notice first when test riding a very expensive bicycle.

But the right materials are only the beginning of the story. How those metals are fashioned into the actual bicycle tubing can also be a crucial point to consider. While cheaper frames will have tubes that are the same thickness throughout, the better touring bikes will have what is known as "double-butted" tubing. Because the greatest amount of stress occurs near the point where the tubes of a bike frame are joined together, a far superior construction technique is to fashion a tube that is thinner in the middle than it is at the ends. This, of course, saves a great deal of weight, and also adds a great deal to that responsive feeling of the better bikes.

Since there is no way to tell if a tube is double-butted merely by looking at it, keep your eye open for a decal that states this to be so. (It's highly unlikely that a tube would be double-butted and not have a decal, and don't trust a salesman who tells you otherwise.)

You may hear a lot of discussion regarding whether the frame was joined with or without the use of "lugs." Some quality builders prefer to join perfectly mitered frame tubes together with a thin bead of brazing metal, a process that offers a secure bond without subjecting the metal to the high, stressful temperatures of welding. Other builders, however, join the frame tubes using "lugs." These are simple metal sleeves into which the frame tubes are inserted, and then filled with brazing material.

FRAME JOINTS

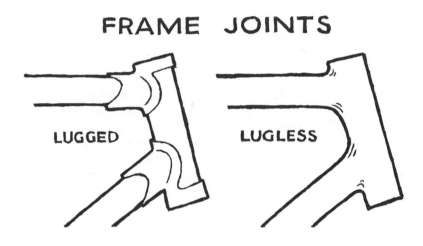

If each process is done well, there is probably no clear-cut winner between lugged and lugless frame construction. Lugged is more commonly seen, perhaps one reason being that it does not require the same precision as lugless construction. The results of either process should form one of the major focal points in your examination of a bike frame. On a lugless frame, the joints should form a smooth, even taper, with no evidence of stray folds or globs of brazing material. On a lugged frame, pay particularly close attention to the places where the metal sleeves join the frame. Have they been filed into clean, 90-degree joints, or are there globs of paint or brazing material at the junctions? Looking carefully at such areas will not reveal if the tubes have been brazed properly, a detail that is virtually impossible to tell just by looking. Such inspections will, however, offer a small clue to the care which the manufacturer has exercised in the production of his bicycle.

What Makes A Touring Frame?

By manipulating certain frame angles and tube lengths, a builder can create a bicycle suited for either racing or touring. There is an incredible difference in the handling properties of the two styles, so much so that you would do well to take a ruler along when bike shopping so that you can be sure just what side of the fence the machine is really on.

For all practical purposes, there are four measurements to be concerned with when choosing a bike for touring:

Length of the chainstay: This refers to the length of the two bottom horizontal tubes that follow along either side of the rear wheel. A racer would tend to use a shorter chainstay, commonly 17 inches or less. This creates a very "stiff" rear end, one that can transfer power to the wheel without swaying back and forth as the bike is pedalled. For the tourist, however, this type of design can cause several problems. First, virtually every bump and grind of the road will be transferred directly to the body, hardly an enjoyable way to spend eight or more hours a day. Second, as the chainstay length is shortened, the angle of the chain as it wraps around the front and rear sprockets is increased, causing harsher shifting. This will be a problem, especially for those who ride with a wide range of rear gear cluster sizes, as is often necessary when traveling through variable terrain.

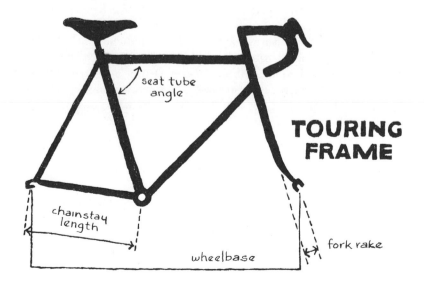

The final problem with a short chainstay is related to the use of rear panniers. When the bags are loaded properly on the rack, you'll usually find that your heels simply don't clear them. In such cases your only choices would be to search for narrow pannier designs or force the bags farther back on the rack—a practice which can decrease the stability of your load.

If touring is your game, look for a chainstay length of 17.5 to 17.75 inches.

Fork rake: This refers to the distance between the main straight tubes on the fork and the center of the wheel axle notches. (Some people simply refer to fork rake as the amount of curve present in the front fork.) Generally speaking, the greater the distance between these two points, the softer the ride. To ensure a minimum of road fatigue to the arms and shoulders, as well as to maintain easy steering qualities, a touring bike should offer a "rake" measurement of around two inches.

Seat tube angle: This is a measurement of the angle formed by the meeting of the seat tube and the top tube. To maximize power transfer, a racing bike will be constructed with a seat tube angle of 74 or more degrees. Again, this is inappropriate for tourists since it produces a very uncomfortable ride on anything but those rarely encountered stretches of perfectly smooth pavement.

Wheelbase: This is the length between the center of the front axle and the center of the rear axle. If your dream bike comes in at under 40 inches, you may want to consider another dream. While a shorter wheelbase may create a responsive ride, it will also buck and snort under rough road conditions.

Use your tape measure and protractor to determine which bikes meet the basic criteria for a touring machine. But then get on each one and ride! A slight variation in any of the above factors can create amazing differences in balance, responsiveness, and steering. Only by riding can you make an intelligent decision as to which frame is going to best suit you over the miles ahead.

What size?

Frame size is one of the most important considerations of any bicycle purchase, but there are practically as many mystical formulas for sizing bike frames as there are bikes to choose from.

One of the most popular sizing theories of all, especially common in Europe, uses inseam measurements. One version states that the distance

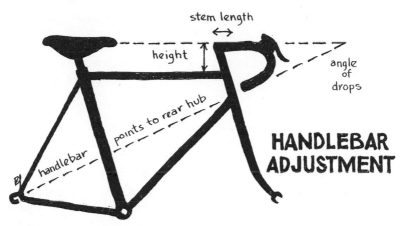

stem length
←→

height

angle
of
drops

points to rear hub

handlebar

B

HANDLEBAR
ADJUSTMENT

from the top of the seat tube to the center of the crank spindle should be 10 inches less than your inseam measurement. This theory fails to recognize that different bikes have different distances between the bottom bracket (and therefore the crank spindle) and the ground. With a high bottom bracket, you could theoretically end up with the proper frame size and still not be able to stand over the bar.

The simplest, safest rule of thumb to use when sizing frames is this: Straddle the frame in flat shoes. You should be able to raise the front end of the bike so that the wheel clears the ground by at least one, but no more than one-and-a-half inches.

Since we're on the subject of proper fit, you should be aware of the fact that you may also have to make adjustments to the saddle and handlebars to obtain optimum comfort and efficiency. Keep the top of the handlebar stem level with the saddle, the nose of which should be tilted slightly upward. (The tip of this nose should be about three inches behind a vertical line running up from the bicycle's bottom bracket.) You'll probably want to experiment a bit with handlebar tilt, but begin by having the drops run along an imaginary line pointing to the rear axle. After riding a bit, you may well discover that you prefer them to be parallel to the frame's top tube instead.

The saddle height should be adjusted so that when you're sitting on it straight, you can just push the heel of your foot against a pedal placed in the 6 o'clock position. Other people go by this rule of thumb: With the front part of your foot properly clipped against the pedal, the leg should be just slightly bent when outstretched as far as possible. It doesn't really matter which of these formulas you use. The point is that having the seat too low will cause you loss of efficiency and painful knee joints, while having it too high can cause leg strain and dangerous loss of control.

WHEELS

Wheels are made up of hubs, spokes, rims, and tires, and, like frames, are of crucial importance to the performance of the touring bike. A wheel is at once one of the most performance-oriented and vulnerable parts of the touring machine. Most of the problems and many of the pleasures associated with riding are directly tied to this component.

One of the most important pragmatic considerations for the long-distance tourist is the proper type of spoke. For most touring applications where panniers will be employed, make sure your spokes are at least 14 gauge. The higher-gauge, lighter-weight spokes are fine for racing, or in some circumstances commuting, but can give you all kinds of fits when you drop a loaded bike on them. Since changing broken rear spokes can be a rather tiresome job—especially if they happen to require the removal of the gear cluster—don't tempt fate by opting for racing gauge.

One method by which you can save on weight without sacrificing spoke strength is to opt for double-butted spokes. The principle here is the same as for frames; the spoke is merely thicker where most stress occurs, namely, at the point where it joins the rim and hub flange.

Though choice of spokes is, like many decisions in the world of bicycling, a matter of weight, the real savings in ounces will be in the choice of hubs and, more importantly, rims. As far as hubs go, you'll often be faced with making a choice between "large flange" and "small flange," which refers to the apron of metal that exists where the spoke attaches to the hub. Large flange offers more strength but a stiff ride, small flange a savings in weight and a smooth ride, but with slightly less wheel strength. Though the support groups for each are well entrenched, there is no clear-cut winner.

Likewise, there is no obvious performance winner between sealed or loose bearings in the hub. Good sealed bearings will allow you to ride more miles before worrying about maintenance (especially if you've been touring in wet or dirty conditions), but you will pay more for this convenience.

The rim is even more important than the hub as far as weight is concerned because the farther away from the axle a wheel component is, the more force is required to get it rolling. Unless you plan on touring on incredibly rough roads or will need to carry exceptional amounts of weight, try to stick to good aluminum alloy rims. Additional strength is gained in the better alloy rims by incorporating hollow structural channels, concave inside surfaces, and the like. Reinforced spoke holes are another sign of quality and will enable you to minimize the effect of the spoke nipples wearing against the inside edges of the holes.

TIRES

Tires basically come in two styles: tubulars and clinchers. Tubulars are also known as "sew-ups," a term that refers to the fact that they are merely lightweight rubber sleeves that are sewn around a tube. They are incredibly light and compact, and they offer the greatest amount of rubber contact with the road. Unfortunately, they are rather more prone to flats on tough terrain. And, once they do go flat, the actual repair process can get quite involved. For racers, they are worth the trouble; for tourists, they are not.

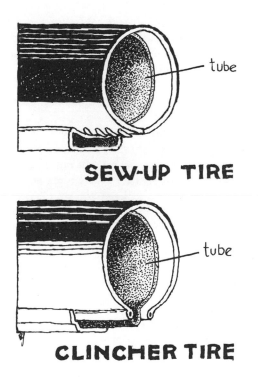

SEW-UP TIRE

CLINCHER TIRE

Touring is substantially easier with a "clincher" tire, more correctly referred to as a "wired-on." While the lower priced clinchers are heavy and cumbersome, the better ones (still about a third the price of a good sew-up) will offer you good wear with a minimum of weight and rolling resistance.

The headaches regarding tires begin when you consider what size to use for touring. The most popular touring tire is still the 27-by-1 1/4-inch. It offers enough contact with the road so that you can ride over light gravel and wet spots without fear of slippage, yet it is not heavy enough to become a real burden. Over the last several years, though, there has been a substantial move toward what are often referred to as "narrow-profile" clinchers. These are still 27 inches in outside diameter, but are only 1 1/8 inches or even 1 inch wide. The theory, as you might have guessed, is to reduce both weight and rolling resistance while keeping the easily maintained clincher style. And, in many ways, these narrow-profile tires have done just that. Unfortunately, for most touring applications, you will notice a substantial loss of control and grip on any uneven, soft, or wet surfaces—not a comfortable thought with a fully loaded bike.

The narrower tires do make a noticeable difference in ride and might be worth considering if you are an experienced cyclist who intends to travel with small or no loads on good roads. Just remember that while a 27-by-1 1/8-inch tire will fit on a 27-by-1 1/4-inch rim, a 27-by-1-inch tire will not. There are special narrow rims for both these sizes of tires, and they are well worth the extra expense for cyclists fitting the above riding profiles.

If you're going to be traveling abroad, you will probably want to switch to 700C tires and rims. These are the foreign equivalent of 27-by-1 1/4-inch tires, though *the two are not interchangeable*. If you keep them on the bike when you return to the United States, you'll have to depend on the better bike shops to keep you supplied with tires and rims of this size. In an emergency situation in many North American locations, you could find yourself a long way from the world of 700C.

GEARING

Yes, there are cliques of cycle-holics who sit in dimly lit barrooms and nearly come to blows over what comprises the ultimate gear range. Perhaps one day you'll wish to join them. But for now, try to gain a basic understanding of this most complicated of all cycling concepts, and learn how to use it to make your long-distance treks more enjoyable.

A 10-speed is so called because two front sprockets can be combined with five rear cogs for a total of 10 gears. Add a third front sprocket and you have three combinations of five for a 15-speed. If you instead add a sixth rear cog, you'll have two front sprockets combined with six rear cogs for a 12-speed. So far, so good. The confusion comes when you start to consider just how those chainwheels and rear cogs relate to each other and what those relationships mean to you when you're trying to maintain a cadence over hill and dale.

The first step in decoding the useful numbers hidden in your drive train is to assign to each cog and chainwheel a number that relates to its size. The formula commonly used in America for determining these numbers has some rather archaic ties to yesterday's old high-wheelers, which had pedals directly tied to the front wheel. Let's suppose that you hear someone say that their 10-speed has a 40-inch gear. This really means that a single revolution of the pedals will take them the same distance as it would on a high-wheeler with a 40-inch front wheel. (Though it would be hard to think of a more obscure measurement, take heart. This gibberish of numbers can take on some real significance if you'll hang in there.)

To assign the appropriate figures to your gears, plug the proper numbers into this formula:

$$\frac{\text{number of teeth on front chainwheel}}{\text{number of teeth on rear cog}} \times 27 \,(\text{wheel size}) = \text{"gear inches"}$$

Thus if you count the number of teeth on one of your front chainwheels and find them to total 52, and one of your rear cogs, contains 20 teeth, the combination can be expressed in "gear inches," like so:

$$\frac{52}{20} \times 27 = 70.2 \text{ gear inches}$$

Remember, this number—70.2 inches—is essentially an arbitrary figure. Only when it is put into combination with other gear numbers does it take on any real significance. (For what it's worth, you can multiply this figure by pi [3.14] to arrive at the number of inches the bike would travel for every complete revolution of the pedals.)

If you were to use this formula for each of the 10 combinations on your bike, you'd end up with a group of figures that would probably range somewhere between 20 and 100. An "ideal" gearing combination is one that jumps from one gear to the next in *even* progressions without the need for "double-shifting"—that is, having to shift both the front and the rear derailleur to make the next highest or lowest jump. To do this is, I'm sorry to report, impossible. Once you've swallowed that sad truth, you can get down to the business of either working your riding cadence into your current gear progressions or changing them to better suit your needs.

It's beneficial to talk first about the end gearing extremes—how high is high enough, how low is low enough? For an individual in "average" shape intending to ride in the mountains, a low-end gear in the low- to mid-twenties would probably be sufficient. On the other hand, if you plan to ride only on flat lands or are in incredible shape, you might want to jump up your low gear to the mid- or upper-thirties. By doing this, you would be reducing the spread between the highest and lowest gears and could therefore achieve more even "steps" when shifting from one gear to the next. Many cyclists, though, have a real preference for a low "granny gear" that can get you up those long hills with a full load. Ultimately, the only way you'll know if your gears are low enough is to get out there and try them—preferably, long before you're off and running on an actual trip.

As for the high-end gear, most of the standard gear sets you'll run across top out at around 100. While this is fine for trying to become air-borne down steep grades, you'd do well to consider lowering this to something in the low- to mid-90s. Again, this is to reduce the gear spread for more even shifts between the middle and upper ranges. The low- to mid-90s will do fine for nearly all situations other than mountain racing, while allowing for a smoother transition between the middle- and upper-range gears.

For all our efforts, perfectly spaced gear jumps are simply not possible. More than likely you'll have combinations that range from five- to fifteen-inch jumps. Most cyclists prefer to have the most consistent spacing (in six- to ten-inch progressions) either in the low end or middle range. The strategy for the former is that when going up steep grades, you'll want a shift that can be made smoothly and without disruption of cadence. The latter preference states quite correctly that since you will do most of your riding in the middle ranges, here is where your greatest concentration of smooth shifting should be. Both schools of thought have a lot of merit; only riding each type will help you decide which is right for you.

Keep in mind that although you may be riding a 10-speed, there are really only eight acceptable gear choices. The two combinations that you should avoid are when the chain flows either from the outside rear to the inside front, or vice versa. Both of these create a tremendous amount of wear and tear on the chain and, more importantly, on the softer alloy teeth of the front chainwheels. On most bikes, you'll be able to feel and hear the extra grinding going on when riding in either of these gears.

One way to increase the choices available for smooth shifting is to increase the number of rear wheel cogs to six, instead of five. At one time this created problems because a cluster of six gears took up more space than did five, which caused headaches in everything from the construction of the rear wheel to the shifting ability of the derailleur. Now, however, there exists a system that has managed to put six gears into the space that normally held five. The result is a clean shifting system that is worth consideration by those frustrated with their current range of gears.

Another option that may seem attractive at first is to add a third front chainwheel and create a 15-speed bicycle. There are, however, some real drawbacks to this. First, by moving the chainwheel farther out from the frame, you create considerably more whip and add stress to the frame. Additionally, there is a great deal more wear on the outer chainwheel. If you do elect to go with 15 speeds, you'll also have to add a derailleur that has an extremely wide range (usually with a loss of clean shifting ability). The only people who will probably find the advantages of 15 speeds to outweigh the disadvantages are those who need to routinely climb extremely steep grades and cannot handle more traditional 10-speed "granny gears." If at all possible, ride a 15-speed before you go to the trouble and expense to purchase one or convert your existing machine.

3

Body and Mind

Nothing—not wind, rain, heat, or cold—is more disappointing than to have your trip cut short due to a serious ailment or injury. Sometimes these things can't be helped. But far too often, it's the cyclist himself who unknowingly sets the stage for an incapacitating medical problem. While far from being a carte blanche to good health, proper riding habits and techniques and a short pre-ride stretching routine will go a long way in providing you with thousands of miles of healthy riding.

RIDING HABITS AND TECHNIQUES

Since we're not as concerned here with absolute efficiency as with avoiding damage to your highly breakable body, there are really only a few simple practices that you should adapt to your distance-riding habits. Starting from the bottom, let's talk about toe clips.

First, write down all of the negative things that you've heard about them on a piece of paper. Next, use this list to line the bottom of your bird cage, hamster pen, or kitty litter box—that's really about all it's good for. Toe clips, above all else, ensure proper placement of the foot upon the pedal. Not only does this make riding a lot easier, but it significantly reduces the likelihood of injury to the Achilles tendon and the various ligaments and tendons of the knee. In addition, toe clips allow you to lift the pedals on the upstroke, thus relieving pressure on your feet. USE THEM RELIGIOUSLY!

Speaking of feet, one of the best ways to avoid problems with them is to use cycling shoes. Oh, I've used tennis shoes on some very long trips too, but the additional pressure and strain this causes on the bones and nerves of the feet are really an unnecessary risk to health. As discussed in Chapter 4, opting for a pair of lightweight cycling-walking shoes may be preferable to the cleated hard-shelled shoes that racers use. I will say, however, that if you don't mind the extra weight, cleated hard-shelled footwear is worth your careful consideration. Such shoes are the ultimate means of transferring the effort involved in hill climbing to the proper leg muscles. And as far as getting cleated feet out of the clips, well, that takes about as much skill as it does to unfasten a seat belt.

The number-one fault of most beginning cyclists is their obsession with high gears. Have you ever seen a road racer cranking it out in a slow, hard cadence for very long? The faster spin found in lower gearing not only saves an incredible amount of energy, but is about the best insurance against developing problems in the lower leg and knee areas. It's especially important, from a medical standpoint, to use lower gearing when climbing hills. Should you not heed this advice, you could one day be faced with the unpleasant necessity of staying off your bike for a very long time while your strained tendon or torn ligament heals or while you have it repaired by a surgeon. If you do nothing else different on your next trip, please—stay out of tenth gear.

If you happen to notice any pain on the inside or outside of your knee, check to make sure your legs are not tilted in or out when riding. If you see a problem, it will take a conscious effort to change your leg alignment if you've been riding that way for very long. But by all means do it, if you want to avoid serious ailments later on.

Another problem sometimes encountered in long-distance riding concerns the hands. Hardly anyone has gone on a long ride without feeling some numbness, but ignoring this situation for prolonged periods can sometimes result in damage to the nerves. I assume you already have gloves, so the next step to relieve the problem would be either to apply a foam rubber handlebar covering or to layer-wrap thin strips of padding material around your bars, secured with tape. Even with all this effort, it's a good idea to lighten your grip, change hand positions once in awhile, and where it is safe to do so, remove the weight from your hands entirely for brief periods.

Moving inward from the hands, we come to saddle sores. While these can cause terrific problems, they are usually preventable. Chafing of the skin is the cause of such maladies, and sweating makes matters worse in a hurry. Always wear clean riding shorts, and apply a liberal amount of plain talc powder to the inside of them at regular intervals. If you happen to have some excess baggage on your upper legs, sprinkle a liberal amount on the insides of your thighs, as well. You may look like a flour bomb just went off in your shorts, but you'll feel great. If you do develop a rash or sore, clean the area with medicated soap, dry thoroughly, and apply talc. Don't use creams or lotions, as they can actually aggravate the condition further.

STRETCHING

Of all the suggestions for healthier riding in this chapter, stretching is probably the one that you'll be most tempted to ignore. Don't! If you keep at stretching, it will make a big difference in your performance and significantly reduce the likelihood of muscle strains and tears. The following stretches should be used in a 10-minute routine before each riding session.

Shoulder stretch: While standing upright with feet spread about 18 inches apart, clasp your hands behind your back. Keeping your arms straight, bend forward while slowly raising your arms as high as possible

STRETCHES
FOR
CYCLISTS

SHOULDER STRETCH

NECK CIRCLES / BACK PULL

FLOOR TOUCH

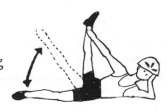

LEG STRETCH

SIDE STRETCH

over your head. Hold for five to ten seconds. Return to upright position and repeat four or five times. Don't overstretch!

Neck circles with back pull: While standing upright with feet slightly spread, move your head forward slowly until your chin rests against your chest. Now rotate your head in a smooth, slow circle, being careful not to move your shoulders. After one revolution, return your head to an upright position. Now try to pull your shoulder blades together. Hold for five seconds and release slowly. Alternate between neck circles and upper back contractions until you have completed four of each. Alternate direction of the neck circles. (This one is especially good for relieving riding fatigue.)

Floor touch: Stand with feet spread apart about 24 inches. Then bend over and touch the floor with your hands, wrists, or even forearms, depending on what is comfortable. Hold this position for three or four seconds and return to an upright position. Repeat five times.

Leg stretch: Lie down on the floor propped up on your left elbow, feet together. Keeping your legs straight, grab your right ankle with your right hand, and lift the leg to as near a vertical position as possible, toes pointed. This stretch can be enhanced by then raising your left leg up to meet the right, holding for three or four seconds, and releasing. Alternate between legs, four times each.

Side stretch: Sit on the floor with legs straight and spread as wide as possible. Point toes. Grab left ankle with left hand and bend at the waist toward the left foot—do not twist. Right arm should be overhead, straight and parallel to the leg, with palm turned up toward ceiling. Hold for 15 seconds, repeat three times for each side.

If you're so inclined, an easy stretching routine *after* a good ride is also helpful, especially early in your training. Remember, the object here is not pain. If you feel any, you're overdoing it. After riding for a long time, it also feels great to stretch wrists and ankles from side to side, as far as it is comfortable.

One final note: stretching is not to be used in place of a regular training program. The only way to develop the muscular and aerobic skills you need for a long trip is to get out there and ride! Stretching just makes you feel all the better while doing it.

CARE FOR CYCLING INJURIES

The following minor injuries should respond fully to the treatments prescribed here. If they don't, you probably have a more extensive problem than you had at first thought. In such cases, see a doctor as soon as possible. With muscle, ligament, and tendon injuries, even when the wound appears to be healed, tape the affected area with an elastic bandage for additional support, ride only in the lower gears, and reduce your daily mileage until you are back to full strength. Remember: Pushing too hard or too fast will almost certainly leave you unable to ride for a much longer period of time than did the original injury.

Cramps: Cramps can result from mere fatigue or from the loss of potassium and magnesium through sweating. The most common location for cramping is in the legs, and quick relief can be obtained by pointing your toes and stretching the leg as far as possible. Spread a bit of analgesic balm over the affected muscle before riding again.

Strained muscle: Apply an ice pack and pressure bandage to the affected joint for one to two hours. The most important thing to remember with this type of injury is to stay off of it! Get a room or a comfortable campsite as soon as possible, and keep the limb elevated. If the initial cold pack fails to do the trick, continue such treatment for 24 to 48 hours. If there are mountains to climb in the immediate future, either figure an alternative way across them, be willing to walk (depending on the injured joint), or expect to hole up for several days before continuing. By the way, almost all such strains can be avoided with a simple stretching routine.

Pulled muscle or tendon: This is a condition that demands careful attention, since it's often impossible to tell if the muscle or tendon is merely pulled or if it has actually been torn. Once again, get off the injured limb immediately. Apply ice and a pressure bandage for at least three days. As the condition improves, treat it with heat and massage, and rest the limb until all pain has disappeared. This one requires a lot of TLC when you do eventually resume riding. Pray that if it happens to you, you'll be heading east across Nebraska with a strong west wind. ("Should I have stretched?" you ask. You've got it!)

Blisters: There is really no reason you should ever get a blister, but if you do, don't puncture it. This just increases the likelihood of infection. Instead, pad it with a sterile bandage and moleskin, and it will eventually heal itself. In the meantime, find out what caused the problem and correct it.

Something in eye: This is a very common problem, especially for cyclists who wear contacts. I highly recommend wearing sunglasses whenever practical. As your mother undoubtedly told you 100 times, if you do get something in your eye, don't rub it! If you're wearing contacts, remove the appropriate one, clean it thoroughly, and reinsert. If that's not the problem, with a mirror or with someone's help, pull the eyelid back gently and try to locate the particle. If it is resting on the lower lid, roll the lid back and wipe the piece out with a sterile swab. If under the upper lid or on the eyeball, pull the upper lid over the lower one to produce tears. This should wash the particle away. If not, cover the eye with a sterile pad and see a doctor as soon as possible.

MENTAL HASSLES

The effort involved in planning a long-distance cycling trip is usually abundantly fueled with anticipatory energy. Your head is on the road long before your body. Maps and equipment litter the living room floor, and visions of wheeling down the open road fly unfettered, from the time of your morning bowl of Wheaties to the 10 o'clock news. The bigger your trip, the higher your kite. The last thing in the world that you will remind yourself to pack is a good attitude.

Hold it. I know what you may be thinking. These pages of the book are not for you. You've been cycling before. Who needs a stint on the couch to have fun on the road? Please, humor me. If you've never before been on an extended trip—one of three weeks duration or longer—read on. Like the shorter trips you've taken, there will surely be times when you curse the day that Karl von Sauerbronn ever thought up the stupid idea of a bicycle. There may be wet days, hot days, cold days, and uphill days.

But the big difference on a long trip is that these problems aren't just oddities to contend with for brief periods of time. They, along with the anticipation of them, become a way of life. The third day of endless headwind will not be mellowed by homey thoughts that you'll soon be popping beer tabs and watching Star Trek reruns again. For perhaps weeks, or even months, home will be that thin white line, two pairs of chamois shorts, a superfirm mattress, and for dinner, the "one-burner blues." And even though you may not mind inclement weather and harsh terrain, there will probably be a new problem knocking at your brain: boredom. You thought it was a long *drive* through Kansas? You ain't seen nothin' yet! For those going on a long tour for the first time, boredom is probably the least expected complication of all. And if it is not somehow reckoned with, it can set the stage for severe lapses in spirit when you're hit with long stretches of rain, wind, or heat.

But enough horror stories. Obviously, long-distance bicycling is not for everyone. When you complete an extended tour, it is an accomplishment of which you can be proud. Now let's get on to the nitty gritty. How can you keep spinning that crank for 800 more miles, when you'd give anything to be somewhere else?

Dodging the Doldrums

Most psychologists will tell you that when you're feeling the nine-to-five doldrums, it helps to do something to add a little zest to your life—perhaps "get away from it all," even if only for a brief period of time. But when the bicycling blues of a long trip hit us, we are *already* getting away from it all. Nevertheless, the basic philosophy will still work. The mistake that many cyclists make in planning long bike trips is to put themselves on a much too rigid schedule. Then if bad weather sets them back a bit, they feel pressured to make up for lost time. This is one of the quickest ways to bring yourself down if you've still got a lot of road ahead of you. An even worse situation results if you happen to injure yourself, since you may not be as likely to let things heal properly before sprinting off for the finish line.

The point, then, is this: Plan your daily mileages on the low side, with a generous number of layover days. When you feel like riding farther, do so. Just don't leave yourself with a 125-mile ride to reach the next stopover point. (As mentioned in Chapter 9 on "Heat," don't exercise this option at all when riding in very hot, desolate regions. There, no matter how good you feel, stop on schedule.)

Depending on how much you've trained for your trip, allow seven to ten days of riding before expecting to feel really "into" the routine. Assuming terrain factors to be constant for a one-month trip, plan daily mileages for the first third of the trip to be about 20 to 25 percent lower than the latter two-thirds. Put some extra effort into researching points of interest along the final 200 miles of your route. That way, if you haven't used those extra days you put into your schedule, you can still enjoy the full amount of time allotted for your ride. Even though you may be anxious to get to your final destination, some relaxed sightseeing on the last leg of your route will help you to finish strong.

But let's get back to the problem of variety or "getting away from it all" to rekindle a lagging spirit. First of all, I will assume that most of your budgets would not allow for a jet getaway weekend to Sun Valley for a few rounds of golf. Heaven knows many of us have a hard enough time affording the extra 50 cents for a black-and-white TV at Motel 6. No, mental relief has to be a relatively simple affair for the average cyclist. Following are a few ideas that have worked for me.

Many YMCAs have guest passes for as little as $1, which will allow you to swim, play basketball or pool, and use the other facilities. I prefer to stick to the Y's in medium-sized towns. There I've had somewhat better luck finding ones receptive to nonmembers, and big-city facilities may be far off my intended route. I like to arrive at a Y after a good morning's ride, use the facilities for about three hours, and then ride outside of town to a campsite. Although they cost more, racquetball and tennis clubs will often have guest passes for their facilities, as well. And if your poor body is really dragging, most of these also have whirlpools and saunas.

Eating out is usually a good pickup, especially if you've been cooking most of your own meals. Restaurants with soup and salad bars can fill you up for $4 to $5. How about a movie? Theaters across the country often have "dollar days" or sharply reduced rates for afternoon or early-evening weekday shows. (Don't, however, count on finding these in very small towns.)

You will have discovered long before the blues hit that getting cleaned up helps to lift the spirits. But have you ever tried a haircut? As strange as it may sound, this can make you feel much better. And I know several cyclists, who, after four or five weeks on the road, purchase new T-shirts or "campground wear" to help their dispositions. If you don't think that this is effective, try wearing the same two or three outfits for a month at

home and see how thrilled you suddenly become with that ugly shirt your
aunt gave you for your birthday last year.

It will also help you over mental humps if you can do some things
"off the bike." A day hike in a state park is great. Or leave your bike and
gear at the police station or with a local merchant, and take an excursion
bus to a nearby point of interest. The local chamber of commerce can
probably give you a pannier full of ideas.

Buy a cheap air mattress and spend the afternoon floating on a local
lake. (But be careful of sunburn!) If it's a popular place, there will probably be boats and fishing gear for rent. Go to a school or city league
sporting event. These are usually fairly cheap (sometimes free) and are
super for getting your mind off the road for awhile.

Mail is a great thing to receive on the road. Give your family, friends,
or creditors a list of fairly small towns along your route, along with your
approximate arrival date. Just have them send it to you marked "general
delivery." (The reason I say to use small towns is that larger urban areas
often have more than one post office; you could easily end up looking for
your booty at the wrong one.) If it looks like you're going to be a little late
getting to one of these towns, it's a good idea to call the post office and let
them know that you're on your way. Believe me, there are times when a
seed catalogue with your name on it can make your day. A call to your
family or a friend always helps, and, if done on a weekend, shouldn't
send you to the poorhouse.

A daily journal is about the best no-cost thing you can do to keep
your emotions in check. You can cry and complain until your ink runs

dry, and you will feel much better for getting it all out. This is a hard habit to get into, but I guarantee that you'll appreciate the sentiment—bitter as well as sweet—long after your trip has ended. As a final suggestion for those hard-to-ride days, you and your riding companions should take the time to enjoy a good round of complaining over a cup of coffee.

Handling Hills

For a good case of short-term depression, hills are hard to beat. Some people are determined that even if they stop to rest on a long hill-climb, walking is out of the question. But just because your cycling companion feels this way, don't let it keep you from switching from wheels to feet. It does take about as much effort to walk a loaded bicycle up a steep incline as it does to ride one, but you may just want to slow down and look at something besides that damnable rising white line. When you stop to rest, don't sit down for too long. You may cool down so much that your muscles will revolt against the climb even more than they did before you stopped.

Hills and mountains are truly appropriate places for "management by objectives." Pick out an object up the road from your current resting place, and think only of getting to that spot—no farther. If it's a winding climb, try to make it to the next mile marker, or count off reflector posts. Stop at the scenic overlooks and get a good view of why you hurt so much. For my own peace of mind, I rarely bother looking for the summit, since it's never around the next curve anyway. (For more on mountain riding, see Chapter 12.)

These same techniques can be used in strong winds, with marginal results. After all, there's no trip down the other side to look forward to. I prefer to just stare at the back of my drafting partner, relishing the moments when she's out in front instead of me. For other environmental problems, reduce your daily mileage expectations, be kind to yourself with motel rooms if possible, and consider changing your intended route if the situation is severe enough.

4

What to Take and Where to Put It

To some, it is a disheartening thing to pump that first mile on a loaded touring bicycle. What was once a responsive skim astride a twist of high-tech alloy has suddenly taken on all the charm of a slow plod through a bowl of oatmeal. Those who gave no thought to finger-lifting their machines over curbs now wonder if Blue Cross covers recreational hernias.

But as the road wears on, one does tend to gain a new strength and feel for riding with a load. Pushing 30 extra pounds up a hill becomes almost natural. After 400 or 500 miles, even the urge to ride just one quick bare-bike sprint around the campground seems to fade. But making this happy transition depends almost entirely on maintaining a properly loaded bike. Shifting equipment and improperly balanced front and rear panniers will prohibit you from ever getting a confident, solid feel for the machine. It's depressing and it's dangerous.

LOADING STRATEGIES

With all the different styles and designs of panniers and handlebar bags, it's useless to try to tell you what piece of equipment should go where. There are, however, some definite basics to keep in mind about the loading process. When filling panniers, remember that the heaviest items should be placed low and over the hub of the wheel. Whenever practical, I'm a togetherness person. For instance, rather than cramming my various tools into the little pockets of every pannier and bag, I put all

PROPER LOADING

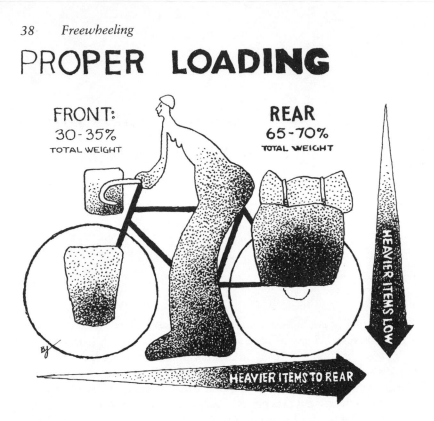

FRONT:
30-35%
TOTAL WEIGHT

REAR
65-70%
TOTAL WEIGHT

HEAVIER ITEMS LOW

HEAVIER ITEMS TO REAR

of them in a canvas stuff sack. Though not bulky, this is obviously a heavy item, hence it gets put at the bottom of a rear pannier.

Though it may seem like an unnecessary hassle to unload an entire pannier to fix a simple flat, it's really not as bad as it sounds. However, if I were getting flats very often, I'm sure I might change my strategy. Many riders prefer to keep a small packet containing a spare tube, tire patch kit, and tire irons where they can get their hands on it very quickly. Other items that might qualify for separate packing would be an air pressure gauge and a spoke wrench. (The roadways of the world are, unfortunately, laced with stretches of bumps and grinds, many of which can reshape your rims in rather short order.) A tool like a pedal wrench, which you'll probably need only at the end of the trip if you plan to ship your bike home via a public carrier, can be kept buried and out of the way.

Keep in mind that if you will be riding with others (but not 10 miles ahead or behind them), some sharing of tools can take place. Some riders prefer to split up tools according to function—one with the brake tools, another with wheel and power train tools, and so forth. Just as simple

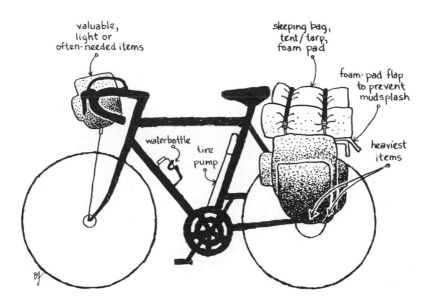

valuable,
light or
often-needed items

sleeping bag,
tent/tarp,
foam pad

foam-pad flap
to prevent
mudsplash

waterbottle

tire
pump

heaviest
items

would be to write down all the repair equipment and parts that you're carrying and keep this list in your front handlebar bag. This way, if someone needs something during those first confusing days, it will be easy to find out who has it.

But back to loading. With tools or something similarly heavy placed low over the right-rear hub, you'll need something of approximately equal weight over the left. The stove or cook set is a good start. Or if your tent is small enough (or your panniers large enough), you could use this for counterweight. The higher you get in your bags, the lighter should be the items you load.

Two pieces of equipment that will almost certainly not fit into a pannier will be your sleeping bag and pad. These should be strapped or bungeed *lengthwise* on top of the rack. Though you will often see them loaded crossways across the rack, loading them in such a manner does nothing but increase your wind drag—just what you need in a Texas blow.

If you don't have fenders, place a cut piece of foam pad over the top of the rack before loading up. This will alleviate much of the usual mud splatter that can cake your tent stuff sack during wet-weather riding. By extending the piece beyond the end of the rack to the edge of the rear wheel, you can also avoid much of the "slop line" that will otherwise decorate the back of your shirt at every cloudburst.

If you're using front panniers, *don't* split the weight evenly among front and back wheels. A 30 to 35 percent front and 65 to 70 percent rear weight ratio is much more ideal. This is such an important concern that you should weigh each bag on the bathroom scale before loading it on the bike. For 30 pounds of equipment, you should have between 10 and 11 pounds per rear pannier side, and no more than four or five pounds per side on the front.

Those things you'll want to be able to get to easily, if not too heavy, can be loaded in your front handlebar bag. For instance, this is where I keep my camera equipment, protected by a cut piece of foam pad that encircles the inside of the bag. Perhaps my windbreaker and sweat pants will go on top for a bit of extra padding. Securing the bag to the front forks with good shock cords alleviates any potential steering problems that a bouncing bag might cause. You should be extremely careful, however, to never overload it. Since the handlebar bag is easily removed from the bike and has a purse-like strap attached, it also makes a perfect place to keep your valuables.

Racks

If you're outfitting your bike with a rear pannier system for the first time, don't underestimate the importance of a good rack. (Cheap ones have the rather unnerving tendency to break on rough roads when fully loaded.) I prefer a multiple strut model made of aluminum, though you'll find that the somewhat heavier steel designs will better survive a bad fall. Many cyclists elect a rack that anchors to the brake bolt instead of the frame, since it is often extremely difficult to keep frame racks from slipping down every couple of days. The bad news is that brake bolt models can make brake adjustments rather difficult. Another alternative would be to go with a frame anchor model, but place a block of notched wood between the rack and the bottom crossbar on the frame. This will eliminate any slippage problems. Be sure to carry the proper tool (often an Allen wrench) to maintain the tightness of the rack bolts to the frame stays.

Try to keep the rear rack sitting perfectly horizontal on the bike. To achieve this on a large-trame bicycle, you may have to go with one of the better racks that come with special adjustment features.

Panniers

Though a hearty stab to the pocketbook, good quality panniers are one thing on which you'll never regret spending money. They will significantly affect the safety and performance of a loaded bicycle and, if given even the slightest bit of care, will last you much longer than many other recreational indulgences you care to name.

Under most touring conditions, enough equipment can be properly loaded into rear panniers and a front handlebar bag to eliminate the need for front panniers. If you absolutely have too much equipment for two panniers, as could conceivably occur on a major trek through extremely diverse climates, by all means get front panniers. But think hard about it first. As mentioned above, however, you should never overload the front handlebar bag to make up for your lack of space. This can cause extremely dangerous steering problems. Either jettison a few items, or swallow hard and shell out the money for a front pannier set.

One person should consider a rear pannier setup of 2000 to 2200 cubic inches. Touring partners can each get by on a long trip with about 1800. There is a sound school of thought that says you'll give into the temptation of filling up the extra space of a big bag. But after one or two good hard trips, you won't be any more excited about stuffing holes than a backpacker is to fill an expedition pack for a three-day summer jaunt. Personally, I'd rather have a bit of extra room for fresh fruit or food bought late in the day for supper, an occasional collection of special camera equipment, or whatever. The choice is yours.

The side of the rear pannier that faces the front of the bike is the one either cut on a slant or with the smallest of the available side pockets. This design feature is so that your heel will have adequate clearance of the bags when you're riding. Just to make sure it all works like the engineers thought it would, though, be sure and try before you buy! (Since panniers should be either centered over the rear axle or slightly forward of this point to stabilize the load, it's not a good idea to obtain needed heel clearance by sliding the bags to the rear.)

Treat pannier seams with a sealer as you would a tent, and line each one with a heavy-duty garbage bag closed with a twist tie. *All* panniers and bags will get moisture in them! You may even wish to put certain equipment in additional smaller bags, especially when riding in areas where rainy weather is fairly common. (Always take extra bags and ties.)

On the road you should make periodic checks of the pannier suspension bolts and nuts to make sure that road vibrations have not jarred them loose. To help eliminate the problem, you can replace the standard flat washers that come on most suspension systems with lock washers.

Handlebar Bags

When choosing a front bag, go with a good alloy or steel support system, and be sure to purchase shock cords for securing the bag to the front fork. The inside of the bag should have good aluminum stiffeners, especially if you plan to carry any fragile items, such as camera equipment.

WHAT TO TAKE

To some of you, the following equipment lists will seem extravagant. And to others, it may appear that I've carelessly eliminated most of the finer things in life. Of the two divergent groups, I would tend to worry far more about the latter.

While it's impossible for the cycle tourist to maintain that airy feeling of bare biking, don't lose any more of it than you have to. By all means try to keep your equipment weight around 35 pounds for all but the grandest of trips. You'll be amazed at how little you can actually get by on. And remember, you can buy equipment on the road if you find you really need it.

Of all the lists, the one for tools will probably seem the most extravagant. Perhaps I carry such a complete set because I'm a secret practitioner of "Zen and the art of bicycle maintenance." Becoming intimately familiar with your bike on a long trip offers a blending of the spiritual aspects of the journey with an appreciation for one of the simplest, most efficient technologies of self-propulsion known to man. Also, a basic knowledge of bicycle repair—which can be gained rather easily—tends to complete the self-sufficient feeling so inherent in this mode of travel.

In short, try your darnedest to carry only as much equipment as you need to sleep well, eat well, and function capably along the open road.

Camping Gear

water containers	tent
tarps and ground cloths	sleeping bag
closed-cell foam pad or	knife
inflatable foam pad	

Worth a closer look...

Water containers: If you're traveling any distance at all, you'll definitely want to carry extra water containers. Besides giving you more capacity on the road (essential in desert environments), extra water containers will make camp cooking much easier because you won't have to run back and forth to the spigot all evening.

If you want something absolutely leakproof and don't mind spending a couple of dollars to get it, go with high density polyethylene bottles. The Nalge Company of Rochester, New York, makes a wide variety of such containers that are guaranteed not to leak. (And they don't, either.) If you plan to carry only water in them, there are several pint-sized juice containers on the market that will suffice. Just be sure to load them so that if they ever do begin to dribble, no serious equipment damage will occur. Though really only practical for campground use, other containers worth considering are the collapsible one-gallon jugs with built-in spigots. These jugs are great for those times when the water supply is located far off, and they can even be elevated and put to use as a crude shower. But if you find that you're pressed for space, this is one luxury that is easily left behind.

Tarps and ground cloths: If you're a dyed-in-the-wool tarp camper, more power to you. You'll certainly save lots of weight, space, and expense over the tenters. With cycling, however, do be prepared for very little privacy, along with occasional barrages of bugs, as well as blowing sand, and rain.

A tarp intended for use as a shelter should be considerably longer and wider than the area required just to cover your sleeping bag. Besides needing room to spread out a bit for cooking, clothes drying, and the like, you may experience a wind shift on a rainy night that will suddenly start throwing water in an entirely new direction. Since reorienting the tarp is obviously a last resort, make sure you have allowed for adequate amounts of "cringing space."

While creating an A-frame shelter with a tarp is best in cold weather if well-aired, open-ended setups can be much better in warmer weather. You'll especially appreciate such an arrangement in hot or humid weather, when you need all the ventilation you can get. While many people use clear plastic for their tarp tents, this is totally unacceptable in desert conditions. Should you need emergency shelter during the day, such material would do nothing but create an oven for you. Heavy white plastic is the best answer for such situations, but you may have to look a few places before you find it. Take plenty of good rope for your tarpitec-

TARP SHELTERS

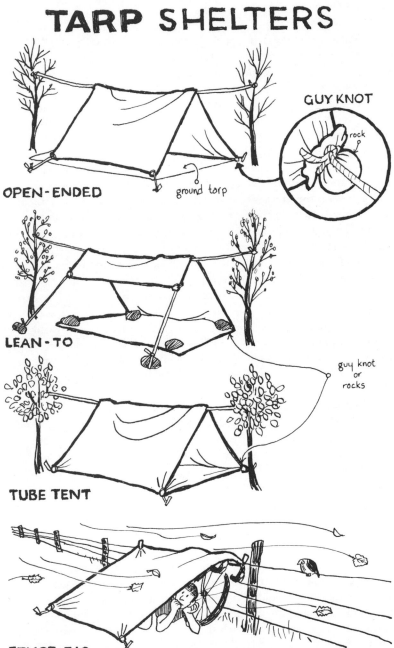

GUY KNOT

rock

OPEN-ENDED

ground tarp

LEAN-TO

guy knot or rocks

TUBE TENT

FENCE RIG

ture projects, as trees tend to grow few and far between when you really need them.

Fasten your guy lines by folding a small rock into the corner of the tarp and tying a simple square knot behind the bulge. A cheap ground tarp to roll your sleeping bag out on should complete your shelter. (Even if you're tenting, you should plan on carrying a ground tarp to lay beneath the tent floor. This will form a good moisture barrier, and your tent floor will last longer if not set directly on the ground.)

An inexpensive option to the plain tarp that can cut down on setup time is a tube tent. These are simple, open-ended sleeves of thin nylon (or occasionally fabric) that will at least provide adequate protection from light rains. You will find that plastic models typically weigh in at around a pound, with fabric at about twice that. While the plastic is of course the less expensive of the two, it often can't be counted on to last for more than a couple of weeks.

One luxury that I add to my load is an additional section of 5-by-8 plastic tarp to cover my bike and my wife's during in-camp rainstorms. Undoubtedly, some people would view such precaution as extreme. But remember: sparing your machine from inclement weather whenever practical will prolong the time between major wheel regreasings. You'll also save on chain and derailleur lubricant, keep your cables sliding well, and prolong the life of leather saddles and cloth handlebar tape.

Another common use for this extra tarp is for quick shelter during a downpour along treeless sections of road. For such use, rather than running around in the rain looking for rocks to use as guy line anchors, buy several of the tarp clips found at backpacking stores. Pack the shelter with lines clipped to the four corners and make sure you can get to it quickly if the need arises. In the desert, creosote, ocotillo, sotol, yucca, and mesquite can be used for anchor points, though you should be careful not to damage the plants in the process. Quite often you'll be riding along a fence line when the skies let loose. Simply anchor the tarp to the top rail or wire, lean your bike against the fence, and pull the shelter over you and the bike. Stake it or secure it to the ground with a couple of rocks, and you're set for the duration. Some people use their tent flies for such emergency shelters, but the occasional need to retreat into thorny plants, sharp rocks, or barbed wire makes it worth the extra couple of ounces to carry a separate piece of plastic. When it gets ripped up, lay out a dollar or two for another.

Tents: Besides the blessed protection they offer from bugs, tents can provide you with a womblike feeling of security on long trips of continuous camping. Don't get me wrong—it's great to lie out in the wide open spaces and stare at the stars. But just as often, cycle camping will place you in public campgrounds, staring instead at the peering eyes of circling motor home jockeys. A tent can be a beautiful, welcome retreat.

The current selection of tent styles and prices is overwhelming. Basically, look for one with a waterproof floor that runs partway up the sides. The walls and ceiling should be of breathable ripstop nylon. (No matter how many windows the thing has for ventilation, a totally waterproof tent can leave you wet from inside condensation.) Some sort of waterproof fly should cover the shelter, leaving a space between for moisture to escape before it condenses on the fly and drips back down. The alternative to this would be to investigate the newer single-layer tents that use Gore-Tex or some similar material for the walls and ceiling, thus eliminating the need for a fly. If at all possible, however, try out one of these tents before you buy to make sure that you have no problems with inside condensation. Also, be aware that many such materials require you to launder them very carefully and frequently if they are to continue to perform properly.

Be sure that the tent is roomy enough to comfortably house all of its occupants and, if desired, some of their gear. Spending a rainy day in a tent that's barely big enough to turn around in can start some people climbing those ripstop walls in no time. Should there be two claustrophobics sandwiched into such a situation, warfare is almost inevitable.

Other items that the long-distance cyclist should be concerned with are the tent poles. No matter how light the shelter is, 24- or 30-inch poles will severely limit where an otherwise compact tent can be loaded. Either steel or aluminum stakes are acceptable. Though aluminum bends more easily, maintaining a sharp point on them with an occasional filing will allow you to pound them into some very hard ground—the kind you'll often find in public campgrounds. In a real pinch, broken coat hangers will suffice if the ground will yield to them.

If your tent is packed outside of your panniers, put it in an extra stuff sack. If you drop the bike while going fairly fast, this will keep road abrasion damage to a minimum. This practice will also allow you to fill one of the stuff sacks with a piece or two of clothing and use it for a pillow at night.

Though a good tent will last a long time if properly taken care of, don't feel like you have to spend a fortune on one. You'll probably be cycle camping in fairly moderate weather, and a cheap tent that meets the above criteria can serve you for many seasons. Just be prepared for little annoyances, such as zippers that easily rust or become clogged with dirt, fragile mosquito netting, a lack of nylon collars to keep out blowing sand, and so forth. If you want to be able to camp often in adverse conditions, such as during high winds or blowing rain, you would do well to move up to the better tents that are specially designed to handle such conditions. The tent's profile, methods of staking, and presence or absence of window collars are just a few things that will give you a clue to the designer's concerns when he developed the structure.

During the trip, try to avoid keeping a wet tent rolled up in warm weather for very long, as this rapidly promotes mildew. Upon returning home, set up the tent and hose it out thoroughly, and reseal the seams after each season of use. If special cleaning instructions are provided by the manufacturer, follow them to the letter.

If you don't mind cramped quarters, the bivy sack is a wonderfully lightweight alternative to standard tents, especially for solo riders. This is basically a cover that envelops the occupant, consisting of waterproof nylon on the bottom and a breathable material such as Gore-Tex on the top. Some models come with a section of screening for added ventilation. Since inside storage space is virtually nonexistent, you will probably want to make sure that you have an additional lightweight tarp to cover any camping equipment vulnerable to inclement weather. Keep in mind that many people do not report satisfactory results when using bivy sacks in consistently rainy weather.

Sleeping bag: This is absolutely the most important part of the cyclist's camping ensemble. A good night's sleep is essential to enjoying (or at least enduring) whatever comes along the white line the following day.

As for whether you should use a bag filled with synthetics or down, the choice is strictly up to you. Down costs more, but it compresses into a smaller bundle—a big advantage for the camping cyclist. Lining your stuff sack with one or two heavy-duty garbage bags should keep the down from ever getting wet, so forget the horror stories about rain-soaked goose feathers. I've toured a very wet Olympic Peninsula in Washington State with a down bag and never had a bit of trouble. (I would never, however, tour in wet climates with a down bag and only a tarp for shelter.) If money is more of a problem than bulk, or if you plan to do extensive canoe or snow camping, go synthetic.

Whatever kind of bag you choose, check for such things as heavy-duty zippers, stitching quality, and how the fill is anchored (slant box—best; offset quilting—good; through-stitched—poor). A mummy style is not only the most efficient for retaining body heat, but will also stuff into the smallest bundle. If you're new to the sleeping bag jungle, limit your shopping to good name brands at reputable shops.

If you're like most cyclists, your bag will be accompanying you on occasional backpacking trips as well. If you can afford two bags, one for cold alpine conditions and one for moderate cycling conditions, you're indeed one of the fortunate few. For most of us, one bag has to pretty much fill all of our needs. I suggest that you get a bag that will perform under the coldest conditions in which you plan to use it. Then for cycling in warm climates, just take a cotton bag liner and use it for your cover. Besides being very comfortable, these liners will keep your bag clean much longer and are easily tossed into the wash with the regular laundry. Also, if in moderate climates you plan on sleeping in a bag rated for very cold temperatures, be absolutely sure that it has a two-way zipper system so that you can get ventilation from either end.

Clothing

bicycling shoes	sandals or moccasins
bathing suit	underwear
cycling gloves	cycling shorts
socks, 2 pairs	long pants, 1 pair
rain gear	2 or 3 tops
bandana (good for potholder, washcloth, etc.)	sweat pants
	hat
windbreaker	lightweight wool sweater

Worth a closer look...

Bicycling shoes: To many riders, the traditional cleated racing shoe is the only game in town. And understandably so. Totally unlike standard jogging shoes, they transfer all of the power directly to the crank and prevent rat-trap pedals from pushing painfully into the bottoms of your feet. Since for all practical purposes they can't be walked on, however, you must resign yourself to the weight and bulk of another pair of shoes for camp use or sightseeing.

A perhaps more perfect solution is to go with one of the lightweight "combination" shoes that began hitting the market in the late 1970s. These are basically tennis shoes, with stiff soles and uppers. They allow a painless power transfer, while being quite comfortable for walking.

Bathing suit: You'll need some sort of bathing suit if you plan to take advantage of any public pools along your route. Usually you'll be allowed to take the plunge with "surfing shorts," which can also double as street wear. In most pools, however, cutoff jeans are taboo.

Gloves: Though somewhat expensive, cycling gloves are absolute essentials. You'll need them to clean glass from your tires while riding and relieve pressure on the nerves in your hands, plus they'll save you lots of skin if you take a dive on the road. Take along a couple of needles and some thread for repairing the padding stitches that invariably come loose during extended trips. (You might even want to reinforce these stitches on a sewing maching before you leave.)

It's also a good idea to take along a pair of inexpensive cotton gloves to wear over your cycling gloves and keep your fingers warm on cool mornings. Some cyclists also wear them to keep their hands clean when making bike repairs or working around camp.

Socks: Blended wool wears well and will keep you fairly warm during periods of cold rain. If you don't care to take a cheap pair of gloves for those cold morning rides, an extra pair of wool socks can be used over your cycling gloves with fair success.

Rain gear: See Chapter 7 for information on wet weather riding. Only experience will allow you to decide just how much and what kind of protection feels right.

Windbreaker: A nylon windbreaker is very nice for keeping out downhill chill or very light rain. A good idea, suggested by Tim and Glenda Wilhelm in *The Bicycle Touring Book,* is to sew in pieces of mosquito netting under the arms for increased ventilation.

Sandals or moccasins: Many people consider extra footwear to be an extreme luxury. But even if you choose to make an extended trip in running shoes (which I do not recommend for the sake of the nerves in your feet), a nice, crushable pair of moccasins can feel like heaven after a hot day or a cold soaking on the road. Sandals are a somewhat less comfortable, though much cheaper, alternative.

Underwear: Since underwear is not worn under cycling shorts, two or three pairs for off-hours should be sufficient.

Cycling shorts: I can't emphasize enough the importance of paying careful attention to the one thing that comes between you and your bike. A quality pair of specially designed riding shorts is impossible to beat for comfort and ventilation. Some riders prefer light wool chamois shorts, and, without a doubt, these are probably the most comfortable. The biggest drawback with them is that they do require very frequent washing if infective bacteria are to be kept to a minimum. (While you may hear that chamois can be only handwashed, this is not always true. With some brands, a very gentle cycle on a commercial machine will work fine.) Most manufacturers recommend that chamois shorts be treated with chamois fat after each washing, but you'll probably find that you can occasionally skip such treatments with no adverse effects.

An excellent alternative to the care and feeding of chamois would be to go with cotton shorts lined with terry cloth or felt. If you're ambitious, you can even make such cycling wear yourself from cutoff pants or walking shorts. To avoid chafing, however, make absolutely certain that there are no seams in the material that will come in full contact with the saddle.

Long pants: Though sweat pants are great for in-camp use, long pants are often necessary if you plan to eat in nice restaurants, attend cultural events, and the like. Dress jeans and corduroys are somewhat heavier than other materials, but can be folded in half and rolled tightly with relatively few wrinkles. If you want something more lightweight that won't crease too easily, synthetics may be your best choice.

Tops: A cotton flannel shirt provides warmth, can be kept pretty much wrinkle-free, and makes a great pillow at night. You may want to go with dark colors for your dressier clothing, as grease can somehow manage to show up on everything by the end of a long trip. As far as tops for riding, cycling jerseys are hard to beat for wicking sweat away, but any lightweight cotton T-shirt will suffice.

Lightweight wool sweater: Besides being very comfortable to wear during cool evenings, a lightweight wool sweater is rather like a small insurance policy. Should you get caught in unseasonably cold and wet conditions while riding, wool covered by a windbreaker can be just the thing to keep your body from chilling to the point of hypothermia.

Tools

tire patch kit	rivet extractor
tire irons	chain lube
6-inch crescent wrench	brake cable (rear)
small screwdrivers (Phillips and	derailleur cable (rear)
regular)	chain links
spoke wrench	brake shoes (especially in
freewheel remover	mountains)
six spokes with nipples	2 tubes
8/10 and 9/10mm wrenches	rag
tire gauge	talc for flats
appropriate Allen wrenches	rim strip
cone wrenches	crank extractor
bottom bracket tools	grease
spare tire	third hand (if alone)
small cable cutters	pedal wrench (if assembling or
	disassembling for shipment)

Worth a closer look...

Tire irons: Though most kits give you three, you can get by nicely with two.

Spokes: Remember that front and rear wheels require different sizes!

Tire gauge: Get one that reads up to 110 or 120 pounds per square inch.

Allen wrenches: These are useful for chainwheels, stem, seatpost, derailleur, tip shifters, and racks.

Chain lube: Lightweight, silicon-based oils are excellent.

Rear brake and derailleur cables: Remember to apply a light coating of grease before installing to prolong life and protect from moisture.

Tubes: Take regular ones for most terrains; though heavy, puncture-proof tubes are very worthwhile if you plan to do much riding in the Southwest deserts.

REMEMBER: NONE OF THE ABOVE TOOLS IS WORTH VERY MUCH UNTIL YOU KNOW HOW TO USE IT!

Recreation

Notebook and pens: Forget those fancy waterproof notebooks. (Why would you want to write in the rain anyway?) Just get a steno pad and a couple of ball point pens and keep them in a zipper-top bag or bread sack. Keep this close at hand for making quick notes, jotting down names and addresses, and so forth. When one notebook fills up, mail it home and buy another.

Hacky Sack or Frisbee: Either of these can be a great physical diversion, especially welcome after long hours on the saddle. You might find a foam Frisbee to be lighter and more manageable than plastic, though performance is equally light with any kind of wind. Hacky Sack, a game in which a small leather pouch is kept in the air without using hands or arms, is especially good for stretching out those leg muscles. And the equipment wouldn't fill up the smallest pocket on the worst-designed panniers.

Cooking

stove	bandana for potholder
fuel canister	plastic bags
pots and pans	foil
utensils	matches
storage containers	soap

Worth a closer look...

Stove: Except in the most special or unusual circumstances, plan to use a stove for cooking your meals. It's faster, won't blacken your pots, and in many wood-stripped areas, is much more environmentally sound. Two basic concerns should guide you in your selection of a stove: weight and the availability of fuel.

If you're going to be cycling outside of North America, kerosene units, though bulky, smelly, and cooler-burning, will probably be your best bet. Even if you have trouble locating pure kerosene on some far face of the world, you can make emergency use of diesel fuel or furnace oil. The biggest problem with kerosene stoves is their need for some sort of primer. Most cyclists prefer to carry tubes of jellied alcohol with them, though using alcohol in liquid form may be necessary if you run out of paste in the boondocks.

The two other most popular types of stoves are white gas and

butane. Butane (a form of bottled gas) is certainly the easiest of all stoves to use. Its main drawbacks are that fuel is expensive, difficult to find outside of the United States, Canada, and Europe, and the bulky cartridges must remain fastened to the stove until completely empty. Butane is also, unfortunately, quite inefficient compared with other fuels. It would be the choice for someone who is touring in fairly well-traveled areas and wants the minimum number of hassles when it comes time to fire up the dinner flame.

As for white gas (also known as Coleman Fuel, Blazo, etc.), it is a clean, extremely efficient fuel that needs no other type of priming fuel. Its biggest disadvantage is its relative scarcity in many parts of the world, including Europe. Many people also regret the fact that it seems you can never buy white gas except in giant containers—totally impractical for a cycle tourist. I have found, however, that if your spare bottle of fuel goes dry, more often than not you'll be able to buy a small quantity of it from someone in a campground. Failing at this, simply look up the name of a Coleman repair shop in any fairly large city. Since these shops always have open cans lying around for testing stoves, most will be quite willing to fill up your fuel canister and charge you accordingly.

Buying a liquid fuel stove with a pump on it is definitely a good idea—especially in cold weather. Though you may still have to use some type of special priming paste, the pump can save you an endless number of headaches waiting for the stove to get hot enough to draw fuel.

Fuel canister: Always stick with high-quality fuel canisters. Saving a few cents isn't worth a thing if the cap leaks or the container splits in a bad fall. Make sure to get one of the pouring spouts offered with most canisters, or much of your precious fuel will end up everywhere except in your stove.

Pots and pans: Whether you opt for a cookset or one or two inexpensive pots from a hardware store will probably come down to a matter of economics. Though there are certain conveniences to be enjoyed with the better cooksets, this is definitely a good area to trim the fat, if necessary. If you decide to go with a kit, don't worry if your stove doesn't fit into it, like the well-designed Svea does. Many other things will, including matches, instant soups and oatmeal, spices in 35mm film canisters, can opener, and dishcloth. Whether fine cookset or hardware stock, keep your selections relatively small and lightweight. (A two- or three-quart pot is sufficient for one or two people.) A nonstick finish is a nice luxury that will allow you to spend a lot less time scraping rice off the bottom of your pot. You will, however, *have* to use a plastic or wooden utensil with such finishes, or they will chip and crack in no time at all. (If you shorten the handles, these too will fit inside the cookset.)

Utensils: One spoon per person. If using nonstick pans, also take one wooden or plastic stirring spoon. You'll need one Sierra cup per person. These will serve as bowls or plates for some meals—just drink out of your water containers.

Tupperware makes a container that consists of a shallow bowl on the bottom, a small plate on the top. These are ideal for two people, though you may occasionally fight over who gets the bowl. The bonus with this kind of setup is that it allows semi-leakproof storage of leftovers, or it can be used to carry matches, seasonings, or instant soups and cereals.

Storage: Use 35mm film canisters for all seasonings. (Special shaker tops are available, but totally unworthy of the price.) Keep as much of your cooking gear together as practical. This will save you lots of time and frustration searching for the pepper each night. As with many of the items involved in a long-distance cycling trip, homemade cotton stuff sacks are great for promoting such togetherness. (An old pillow case cut lengthwise into two sections and sewed up the open sides will provide you with a couple at virtually no cost.) Zipper-top bags or bread sacks are also handy (see "Extra plastic bags" in Miscellaneous section).

Matches: For an unbeatably boring pre-trip job, cut the ends off of wooden matches so that they'll fit in a 35mm film canister. Or if you eat out often, you'll find that many restaurants give out boxes of these mini-matches. Flipping your disposable lighter may seem better, but is really just one more temporary, non-biodegradable bit of convenience.

Soap: A good biodegradable soap can be used on dishes, clothing, body, and hair. (If you use it on your hair, you may want to carry a conditioner with you.) Buy in quantity and put into 35mm film canisters bagged in Ziplocs or in special poly bottles before leaving home. For cleaning pots and pans, a sponge with an abrasive coating on one side will clean better and dry much faster than a dishrag. Store it in a zipper-top bag.

Personal

helmet	sunglasses
talc	toothbrush
biodegradable soap	washcloth
small towel	comb
maps	cleaning rag
lip balm	toilet paper

Worth a closer look...

Helmet: Though there is still a large rift between the cyclists who wear helmets and those who do not, one fact has never been clearer: If you happen to be in an accident (an event which too often has nothing to do with your skill as a rider), your chances of dying or becoming permanently disabled from head injuries are many times greater without a helmet.

If you do decide that your brain is worth saving, don't bother putting your money into a marginally effective helmet. The "strip helmet," for example, consists of a circular net of leather or plastic padded strips and is a common choice among racers. The biggest value of such a helmet would be that it could save your scalp from the abrasion that would occur in a bad slide. On a smooth racing track, this would be the injury most likely to occur. But a tourist's world is one of curbs and car parts and various other protrusions, from which the soft, separated strips of leather or plastic offer virtually no protection.

Another choice in helmets is the rather antiquated "hockey style," which seems to be slowly fading from the cycling scene. This was really the first hard-shelled protection offered to the cyclist, and suffers from some rather poor design characteristics. To begin with, the padding material (when used at all) is rather insufficient to protect the head from anything but the most minor impacts. Also, such helmets offer virtually no evaporative cooling ports and can thus become a nightmare to wear in anything but moderate weather.

A more recent helmet design consists of a circular band of hard shell with four plastic flaps coming together over the top of the head. Such helmets (Skid-Lid is the most popular) do have the advantage of using a special *crushable* foam that softens any impact. The relatively wide spacing between the upper flaps, however, could be a problem if you were to fall in a patch of gravel or loose rock. These helmets typically weigh in at around 11 ounces—certainly not enough to bother even the most sensitive of heads.

Without a doubt, the most popular and effective head gear on the market today is commonly referred to as the "Bell-style" helmet, a name which refers to the company that first offered such a design. This helmet fully covers the head with a hard shell lined with crushable foam. A series of small air holes is strategically placed to maximize the effects of evaporative cooling. These helmets typically weigh just over a pound—not a bad burden for the superior protection they offer.

The most frequent complaint heard about full shelled helmets is that they are too hot. To a great degree, this problem is overrated. True, you *will* notice an increase in head temperature, but if you choose a helmet with some cooling design (Bell and MSR are excellent), temperatures well into the 90s should not pose any real problems. To further add to your comfort, choose a light-colored shell that will reflect the sun. On very warm days, stop once in awhile for a good head soaking; the moisture will dramatically increase the evaporative cooling rate.

Sunglasses: I highly recommend that you wear some sort of eye protection while touring. Dirt, dust, and even small rocks can fly into your eyes at any moment. The situation can be especially bad if you're wearing contacts. (Don't forget your cleaning solution!) Try to get a pair of polarized sunglasses, especially if you plan to do any riding along the coast or over snowy mountain passes. You'll also find that polarizing helps in cutting the morning and evening glare from passing vehicles. A hard case is advised.

Talc (unperfumed): Sprinkled liberally in your riding shorts, this is the best thing since sliced bread. It will remove odors, prevent chafing, and help guard against infection. It can also be sprinkled on tire tubes when changing flats to ensure proper seating.

Washcloth: This can be wrung out after use and carried in an open zipper-top bag.

Miscellaneous

lights
first-aid supplies
extra plastic bags

sunscreen
cleaning rag
odometer (optional)
lock

Worth a closer look...

Lights: Either the C-cell or AA flashlights are fine for campground use, though the smallness of the AA size will save you some weight, as well as allow you to hold the thing between your teeth when both hands are needed. To avoid that entire scenario, get a lightweight lantern with a head strap. On long trips, wrap a couple of spare bulbs in paper and place them in a marked 35mm film canister. While spare batteries can be taken, they're also easily picked up along the way. If you're a bedtime reader, pick up a small alpinist's lantern to hang from the ceiling of your tent.

It's not a bad idea to also include some sort of bicycle light that can be used in cases where you get caught out on the road after dark. (Never intentionally ride after dark. Besides the additional danger posed by traffic, there is often no way to really see the potholes, glass, cracks, and crevices that lie in your path. In addition, there is far more chance of hitting small wildlife at night than during the day.) The kind of lamp mentioned above that straps to your forehead is a tolerable solution. If it proves too difficult to position it correctly on your head, you can often figure a way to strap these lights to your front bag. Whatever kind of vision light you choose, try to make it one that will double for use around camp.

As far as a light to make you visible to motorists, it's hard to beat the ones commonly referred to as "leg lights." These are lightweight cylinders that strap to the lower portion of your left leg. There is most often a white or orange lens visible from the front and a red one from the back. What makes it particularly effective is that the movement of your leg while pedalling causes the light beams to rise and fall, almost as if someone were standing on the side of the road waving a small lantern. Also very effective are the blinking yellow lights that can be clipped to your clothing or equipment. Even if you happen to be stopped *off the road* consulting a map or making an emergency repair, the flash will still warn motorists of your presence.

First aid supplies: Kits are fine, but are seldom complete enough to provide you with total protection. Be sure yours has disinfectant soap, medical ointment, adhesive tape, cuticle scissors, rolled gauze, gauze pads, fever thermometer, antiseptic eye ointment, aspirin, and an elastic bandage.

Extra plastic bags: Zipper-top bags make fine storage bags, but don't bother with the ones found in grocery stores. They have an amazing knack for becoming hard to close and are prone to tearing beneath the closure seam. More substantial ones can be ordered (in quantity) from 20th Century Plastics, P.O. Box 3763, Los Angeles, CA 90051.

Sunscreen: Specific discussions regarding sunscreen and sunburn can be found in Chapter 9.

Cleaning rag: Not to make a big deal about this, but pure, unadulterated cotton works best. Terrycloth (as from old dish towels) will constantly get caught in chain links, derailleurs, and elsewhere. Pure synthetics are often nonabsorbent.

Odometer: Some people wouldn't think of traveling without an odometer, and many others wouldn't think of traveling with one. It *is* great to be able to know how far you've come and, consequently, how far you have to go.

The most traditional type of odometer is the kind that has a small pin that attaches to a front-wheel spoke, and each revolution of the wheel trips a small star-shaped gear attached to the odometer itself.

Yes, you can hear the click, click, click of the thing every time the wheel goes around. Such designs also require that you keep an eye on the spoke pin to make sure that it remains in the proper position and that you are just a little careful not to catch the odometer itself on something. Remember also that most such odometers are not accurate over 20 miles per hour, so the miles chalked up cruising down a mountain will likely be a bit on the shy side of reality.

There have been a few companies that have gone to belt-driven odometers, which at least eliminates the clicking and the problem of inaccuracy at high speeds. If you elect to choose such a model, however, be sure to buy extra belts and take them with you on a trip. It's not so much that these belts break, as that they become stretched relatively quickly and start to slip, giving you inaccurate readings. Make it a habit to routinely compare your odometer readings against highway mile markers. When the odometer begins to come up short, it's time for a new belt.

The latest developments in the odometer field are the LCD (liquid crystal display) readout mechanisms that also offer information on cadence, elapsed time, miles traveled since a certain set time, and the like. Because these gadgets use small electric pulses to measure mileage, they are by far the most accurate, noise-free odometer available. The more elaborate ones also come with a rather stiff price tag (commonly $60 to $100). If, however, you can get by with a simpler unit that doesn't offer such things as cadence readouts, that price can be cut to about $35. The cost of all LCD units has already dropped significantly from the time they first appeared on the market, and the bottom may still be a ways off.

Lock: Unfortunately, there is no lock that even comes close to being perfect. What you choose to use will to a certain extent depend on where you will be riding, as well as how much weight and bulk you can put up with.

Since I don't often tour in large cities, I prefer to use a three-eighths-inch cable with a lock of comparable hasp size. While there are certainly thicker cables (as well as thinner ones), each can be easily severed with a pair of bolt cutters. The same may be said of standard chains, though they have the added disadvantage of increased weight and bulk.

If you decide that you want to foil about any thief who might come along, you have two choices. The first is to go with a three-eighths-inch case-hardened length of chain with an equally formidable padlock. Unfortunately, such a number will typically weigh in at around six pounds—far more than most serious tourists can swallow. Another solution would be to go with one of the "super metals" found in locks like the Citadel and Kryptonite. These typically weigh in at around two pounds and are constructed in the shape of an elongated U. Their biggest disadvantages are bulk and the fact that you are much more limited as far as where, and how much, of the bike you can lock up. (Front wheels, for instance, will remain easy prey.)

Whatever you decide to go with, do go with something. Even cheap locks provide some sort of deterrence, and your insurance company will expect to hear that some sort of security system was in place if your bike gets stolen. If you're traveling with another person, opting for chain or cable will allow you to lock two bikes together.

5

Staying Out of Financial Trouble

That money talks
I'll not deny,
I heard it once:
It said, "Goodbye."
    Richard Armour

At one time, long-distance cycling seemed a sport for those on a budget. How else could you travel so far, see so much, and all the while spend little more than if you were at home glued to "The Price is Right"? But as the popularity of pedal-pushing swept across the country, it began taking in the more affluent, and today we are a melting pot of travelers armed with everything from Carte Blanche to coin purses.

This chapter is not just for the indigent. It is designed to give everyone at least a rough idea of what to expect in the way of expenses, as well as how to cut back on some expenditures so that your wallet can be freed for others.

Unless you're an absolute credit cardaholic, go ahead and take your Visa or Master Charge with you. Perhaps you'll find a terrific gift for someone and will want the store to mail it home. (Most merchants in tourist areas will gladly do this.) Or even more frequently, someone will tell you of a great gourmet restaurant that's the talk of the region—a place you simply *must* try. Simply be aware that once in awhile you're going to want to spend a little extra to reward yourself for a trip well taken. Nothing wrong with that. Believe me, you will have earned it.

One final note: The specific prices mentioned in the following paragraphs were based on the cost of food in early 1984. You should be adequately covered if you simply add 10 percent to the figures for each year that has passed since then.

FOOD

With a little thought, preparation, and creativity, the cyclist can eat rather inexpensively along the open road. But while some trimming of the food budget may be in order, don't *ever* sacrifice a nutritional, well-balanced diet for the few dollars it could save you. Your physical health and mental satisfaction absolutely depend on your being well fed. The following information should give you a general idea of how much to budget for food expenses. If you have a high metabolism and eat great quantities, you may spend more than the figures indicate. Fine. You should find plenty of other suggestions here to help make up the deficit.

Of all the meals to eat out, breakfast will be the cheapest, and often, the most appreciated. I like to break camp on a cool morning, ride for a half-hour or so, and settle into a good hot meal.

Lunch is best kept light and simple. Granola, juice, fresh fruit, cheese, and gorp are classics. Though it is not included in the price schedule below, you may also want a juice or gorp break sometime in the afternoon. This will add another dollar or so to the daily total.

A rider who does not eat out, but instead cooks his meals or occasionally eats cold but unprocessed foods with little or no meat, will be able to get by comfortably on $5.50 a day. Meat will increase that cost to roughly $7.75 per day. If you eat breakfast out instead of cooking it yourself, add $2 to the $5.50 per day figure. Eating dinner out will add

$3.50 to $4. In all these cases, I consider lunch to consist of a high-energy snack rather than a full-blown meal.

So a touring cyclist might construct a weekly food plan something like this: Cook-it-yourself with no meat for four days will equal $22 ($5.50 x 4). Then three days of eating breakfasts out and cooking dinners (only one with meat) comes to $24.75 ($7.50 x 3 plus $2.25 extra for meat). This brings the total weekly food cost to $46.75. Meat dinners all week would bring the total to about $60 (six more meat dinners at $2.25 extra per day).

There are definite ways to cut down on your food bill without sacrificing nutrition:

1. Mail ahead spices, dried onions, peppers, mushrooms, and dried fruit. As discussed throughout this book, mailing ahead—as well as back home—is a great convenience. Call ahead to relatively small towns and inform them of your approximate arrival date. Address the packages to yourself, general delivery, anytown, USA with zip code. If you're going to be later than you had originally informed the post office, it's a good idea to call and let them know you're on your way.

2. Bring enough aluminum foil and plastic bags to last the entire trip. Buying these things in enormous quantities (the only way they're offered) can be an equally enormous stab to the pocketbook. To package foil, tear off as many yards as you might need for your trip and lay the strip flat on the floor. Fold in half lengthwise, and then make four-inch folds along the entire length.

If you run out of plastic bags, simply buy a few vegetables or pieces of fruit in a market that offers produce bags. Double-bag if desired.

3. Choose pancakes or French toast when eating breakfast in restaurants. These are almost always cheaper than omelettes or ham and eggs, and are easily digested on the road. Juice and milk prices are high in restaurants. Try to buy these things in the market instead.

4. Look for all-you-can-eat soup and salad bars. For around $4, you can stuff yourself with good, healthy food.

LODGING

The cost of lodging is incredibly variable. Once in awhile you may get stuck for more money than you had expected to pay. Be prepared for it. Because there is a wide variety of overnight accommodations found in the United States (let alone around the world), you'll have to do some research before you can formulate a realistic lodging budget. The following sources should help you get a good idea of just what you can expect along your intended route. Even if money is no object, go ahead and check out all lodging possibilities—special cyclist campsites, hostels, and bed and board facilities are usually filled with fascinating people.

As you put together your lodging budget, be sure to keep the following questions in mind:

1. What is the weather like? Very harsh weather will make you more likely to opt for motels.

2. Are you traveling through popular vacation areas "in season" or "off season"? The difference in room rates is often 30 to 50 percent.

3. Are there public campgrounds, or are the campgrounds primarily private?

4. Are there hostels in the area? These can be especially important in nontourist areas.

Camping

The cheapest way to camp is to simply ask permission from a farmer or rancher to roll out your bag on his property. You'll receive the best responses if you assure the owner that you won't build any fires. Remember that you may want to have your water on hand already, though most people will let you fill at a nearby spigot. By all means, leave no trace that you camped there; we need to keep all the friends we can get.

There also are, hidden in nooks and crannies across the country, a fair number of free campgrounds worthy of your attention. Most often these will be found in state recreation areas and county parks, though once in awhile a free campground will pop up in a national forest or city park, as well. Your best bet is to consult a copy of *Free Campgrounds, USA,* edited by Mary VanMeer and published by East Woods Press. If your financial solvency will depend on these freebies, it wouldn't hurt to write a letter to an appropriate local agency to verify that the site will, in fact, be open. Include a self-addressed stamped postcard for the return of the information.

The second least-expensive place to camp is in state parks and federal recreation areas. (Government campsites used to be significantly cheaper than they are today, but an increased need for revenue and strong lobbying by private campground owners for competitive pricing knocked them up a couple of dollars per night.) Expect to pay $4 or $5 per night for a standard site. Many campgrounds will have "primitive areas" which should cost you only $2 or $3. The only differences will perhaps be the type of rest room (outhouse versus flush with sink), a longer walk to the water spigot, and fewer or no picnic tables. If a state park has set aside a special area for cyclists and hikers, the sites will almost always be in the primitive section. In such cases, expect to pay about 50 cents per person. You can still enjoy all the park's facilities—all in all, a deal that's hard to beat. (It's always a good idea to write to the state department of natural resources to find out about special discounts in campgrounds for cyclists. Addresses and phone numbers can be found in the capital city phone books at your public library.)

The next rung up (or should I say down?) the lodging ladder comes in the form of private campgrounds. Most will not have any special provisions for cyclists, so the $8 to $12 nightly fee will afford you sewage hook-ups, water, and electricity. I recommend bringing along a toaster, hair dryer, and electric shaver in order to take full advantage of these facilities. You can count on showers and possibly a laundromat, however, which may make the steep fee seem worthwhile.

If you've got enough daylight and energy left, take a look at a private facility before handing over the cash. You'll very likely end up being elbow to elbow with RVs full of hyper kids trying to burn off a sugar rush. (But you will get your own picnic table!) Tarp campers: Don't always count on finding tie-down trees in such facilities, though you may be able to use your neighbor's television antenna. Some private campgrounds really make an effort to provide an aesthetic environment for their guests, but you may have to look awhile to find them. The "sardine management" approach seems far more common.

Hostels

Hostels are relatively inexpensive places to spend the night and can offer fine opportunities for socializing with people from around the world. Prices vary, though $6 or $7 per night for members and $8 or $9 for nonmembers (where allowed) is fairly common. Some will have kitchen facilities, "family rooms," and other amenities, and some will look remarkably like army hospitals. The most important point to remember about hostels is that you'll be expected to provide your own linens. More information can be obtained from the address listed in the Appendix.

Motels

The final option for laying down your head for the night is a motel. Chains such as Motel 6 are fine, but you'll not often be in a town that has one. Much more likely, you'll be staying at a family-run establishment. Off-season will see price wars in any tourist town. After choosing a motel that looks appropriate and finding out the price, be sure to ask to see the room first! There's nothing at all wrong with this practice. After all, you'll probably spend one night out of seven with the luxury of a shower, bed, and television after six nights of cold spigots, hard ground, and someone else's portable radio. You deserve an acceptable room! It's up to you to make sure you get it.

One other point: If it has been raining out, clean off the mud from your tires and frame before bringing your bike into the room. I personally never even bring up the subject of bikes in the room with the manager. If he voluntarily tells you that he doesn't allow it, explain your concern and the care which you will take in protecting the property. If the answer is still no, you may wish to go elsewhere. To save yourself a lot of work, be sure to ask for a room on the ground floor.

If you have credit cards, they are a convenient way to pay for motel rooms without depleting your cash reserves. Take advantage of the sink in a motel room to handwash socks, chamois shorts, underwear, handkerchiefs, and other clothing. If you're worried about drying them before departure time, you can often take them down to the local laundromat and put them in a dryer for 15 minutes. (Understandably, some laundromats won't allow this practice if they're full of customers.) Motels are also great places to totally unpack your disarranged panniers, refold clothes, reseal bags, and dig out the loose change. Such repacking has an inexplicably satisfying effect when you take off the next morning.

IF THE BUDGET GETS BLOWN

If you spend a few hours thoughtfully analyzing your proposed trip, you should be able to come fairly close to predicting what the total cost will be. But even the best intentions sometimes get blown when traveling. Your voracious appetite may lead you to restaurant rack and ruin, as could shipping driftwood souvenirs to all the cousins back in Kansas. Some free souls even go on a bicycle trip knowing full well that they're underfinanced. "I'll make it somehow," they think. "Running out of money needn't be the end of the world, or even the fun." And you know what? They're right! With transportation free (as well as camping, if you ask), the only absolute cost is food. (This is, of course, assuming that you

started your trip with adequate tools and parts.) I'm not recommending that you purposely play financial jeopardy, but if it happens, there are a few things you can do about it.

Cash Advances on Credit Cards

Assuming you're not over your card limit already, this is a simple matter of walking into a member bank with proper I.D. and laying down the plastic. Just remember the steep interest rate you'll be charged if you don't pay the entire bill before the due date. Unfortunately, you cannot purchase groceries on a credit card.

Wiring Money

Ideally, you should go down to your bank before leaving home and let one of the officers know in advance that you may be needing a wire transfer during your ride. He may ask you to set up a code word which will properly identify you when doing business over the phone. If circumstances do in fact require you to make a transfer, handling it through your contact will save you a great deal of hassle and delay. Whereas domestic wires are very prompt (usually within 24 hours), those going to other countries are not. These can easily take four or five days, and mysterious disappearances are far from uncommon.

While we're on the subject of banks, it seems appropriate to say a quick word about traveler's checks. The people on television whose vacations are saved within hours of losing their checks *should* be happy. To waltz away totally uninconvenienced is about as likely to happen as turning a straight flush in Monte Carlo. Far more often, getting traveler's check refunds is at least a minor hassle, requiring *days*—not hours—to iron out. (Even in this country, literally thousands of towns are a long ways from a claims office.)

Cashing Checks

If you bank at a facility with statewide offices, your range for check-cashing is improved considerably. Some banks now even have offices throughout entire geographic regions, which if you ride a lot, can be a distinct advantage. Besides a checking account, try to get a money machine card, since funds don't always run out on a weekday between 9:00 and 5:00. With proper I.D., some banks will still cash out-of-state checks from other banks for a $2 or $3 service charge. Such "benevolence," however, is becoming increasingly rare. Don't count on it! The same may be said for retailers. A few who have yet to be burned badly enough will be glad to cash out-of-state checks, but I wouldn't want to count supper on it.

Hitching a Ride

What happens if there are no hidden nest eggs, no willing friends or relatives, and no more credit left on the plastic? If your schedule is absolutely inflexible, you should consider hitching a ride back home. Hitchhiking with a bike? Actually, it's far from difficult. Of course, you're fairly limited to people with pickup trucks, but there are an awful lot of those running around these days. My wife and I have had to hitchhike several times (with two loaded bikes) due to breakdowns and have never had any real problem. It *is* a hassle, loading and unloading your bike for a long series of short hops to home, but it certainly is possible.

Working

A much more satisfactory method of solving the money crunch is to work. While you'll need a couple of extra days to spare for such a solution, in my mind, it's the preferred way to go. So, how does a busted cyclist wearing funny black shorts and fingerless gloves go about getting employed?

First, stay away from cities. Though undoubtedly there *are* one- or two-day jobs to be found here, they are like looking for needles in a haystack. The one exception to this rule is if you're in one of the few towns with a fair amount of nonunionized truck freight coming in. Docks are often short-handed, and if your luck is good you might be able to track down a position.

How about a temporary job service agency? Admittedly, they present a possibility worth checking into, but it's very difficult to just walk in and be placed the same day. And if you don't have a phone where you can be reached, it could mean sitting around the office all day. Another drawback is that your check won't come until the end of the week.

Small towns are usually much better hunting grounds, as it seems that somebody usually knows somebody who knows somebody who could use a hand. But even with small towns, remember that you may have to do some riding in the evening to find an appropriate place to camp.

The best places of all to find work are on farms and ranches. In the spring and early summer, for instance, the entire western United States seems to need a hand cleaning out irrigation ditches. At the same time, some parts of the Midwest will be getting ready to bail hay.

During July in the Corn Belt, de-tasseling is a task that needs enormous amounts of labor. And as summer rolls on, many people growing hay in the West will welcome an extra pair of hands to help stack bales. If you happen to be good with horses, October cattle roundups are also fair sources for a couple of bucks.

Besides providing positions that you can pretty much drift in and out of, a ranch or farm may provide you a free spot to roll out your sleeping bag at night. I recommend checking in a small rural town as to who might be worth trying in the direction you're heading. This will also enable you to drop a name or two of a town local when you finally reach the farm or ranch itself. To tell the truth, such work is sometimes refreshing even if you don't need the money. You'll probably be meeting some great people, as well as getting a good feel for the locale.

You could easily make $50 in two days by working on a farm or ranch—certainly enough for an entire week of raw food. If you're having

tough luck, you might even suggest working for meals. Often other arrangements can be made once you've proven your ability to give an honest day's labor.

GETTING RIPPED OFF

Though it's incredibly rare, it could happen that you'll end up in a sudden financial quandary because of someone else's itchy fingers. You could lose anything, from a front handlebar bag to the whole darned traveling contraption. As you might expect, this is somewhat more common in large cities than it is in rural areas, though it seems that no place is totally immune to the problem.

Before you leave, make sure that you have adequate insurance protection on your bike *and all related equipment*. There are as many ways of settling bike thefts as there are places of getting bikes stolen. Unfortunately, the outcome is not always so good, as far as the bike owner is concerned. In the first place, many companies will only make the bike and equipment an extension of the homeowner's policy. The problem comes when you try to make a claim on a bike that is worth more than it was when you bought it (very common), and end up getting about a third of what you paid for it because the company depreciates it.

It is sometimes more desirable to find a company that will write a separate rider policy on your bike, especially one that consists of "replacement value insurance." Though this is a little more costly, you will be paid the amount of money required to replace your loss. The trouble is, since stolen bikes are so easy to lose and so hard to trace, you may have to shop around a bit to find a company that will write this kind of coverage. When you do find one, you might ask for a list of people who have actually had stolen bicycle claims, to verify that this company does indeed pay without a great deal of balking. If you plan on cycling in other countries, be sure to check whether or not you will be covered.

There are certain things that you can do now that will make filing a claim a lot easier. Keep the bicycle's serial number somewhere on your person whenever you tour. This way you can immediately notify the police with all the pertinent information. You should also have the phone number of the insurance company's claim center, so that the claim can be processed as quickly as possible. And finally, it doesn't hurt to have a couple of recent color photos of the bicycle. One can be given to police and the other to the company to illustrate that the bike was in fact in good condition.

It's not a bad idea to consider what you would do if your bike did get stolen. What would be your means of getting home? Unless you don't mind hitchhiking, you may want to leave a little slack on the credit card or take extra traveler's checks to pay for public transportation. Always keep your money, identification, passport, and other important papers on you—not on the bike. One solution is to keep all such important items in the front handlebar bag and take this with you whenever you leave the bike. Many front bags now come with shoulder straps, which enable you to comfortably carry them around for long periods of time.

There are several steps you can take to minimize the chances of your equipment getting stolen in the first place. The most obvious would be to take a good lock (see Chapter 4) and to then secure your bike to some very permanent object. (This may, by the way, be one of the first questions the insurance company and the police will ask you.) If at all possible, try to run your chain or cable through the front wheel, as well as the back. If you've got a setup that can handle only one wheel, choose the rear one. If an area looks particularly risky and you have quick-release hubs, you may want to carry the front wheel around with you.

If you're going to eat someplace, try to park your bike next to a dining room window and then request a seat next to it. Some establishments will even be receptive to your leaving your trusty steed in the foyer, though you should always ask first. When running into food stores for snacks or simple equipment, let one person stay with the bikes. And as discussed in this chapter, choose motels that have no objection to your keeping your bike in the room with you.

If you're going to a big sporting event or carnival, it's worth the trouble to find someplace else to leave your bike and equipment. Police stations, warehouses, bike shops, and even small manufacturing plants are good places to try. You may wish to offer a $5 "babysitting" fee for the service, though you'll probably find that most people will decline it.

6

Planning Your Route

Anyone who has made the mistake of traveling with a "plan-a-holic" will probably have a bad taste in his mouth for the whole subject of laying out cycling routes. It's not necessary to know whether tomorrow's eggs will be fried or scrambled, what Podunk's main street will look like, or in which rest stop you'll find relief. Overplanning can indeed take away much of the fun and adventure inherent to long-distance cycling.

But there's another side to the story. When you find yourself on a hair-raising truck route, or there's no room in the inns and campgrounds of that special resort area, you'll surely come to regret that you didn't invest a few hours planning before departure to minimize the hassle factor.

Believe it or not, with the right attitude, it's actually possible to *enjoy* the research and planning phases of the trip. Sometimes it's kind of nice to ride down a beautiful valley and know that the river you're following was once a trade route for early mountain men or that a particular village was a stronghold for the Confederates during the Civil War (or even that the blue line that looks so enticing on the map is actually the truck-infested route to and from the state gravel pile). Few of us have the time or inclination to spend road time reading about historical or other oddities in libraries; so if you want to know, find out before you go.

MAPS

The first step of the pretrip planning phase is to start collecting maps. For years, I rode nearly everywhere with little more than a service-station special stuck in my front handlebar bag, assuming that anything not shown in red or, at worst, blue lines was probably a potholed country lane that would surely end in some corn field. The caution was understandable. Who wants to ride 30 miles—a two-hour investment of time—only to have to turn around and return to the original route? And since some of these side roads beckon in the middle of nowhere, it isn't always as easy as asking the mechanic/geographer at the corner gas station. The solution, more often than not, can be found with adequate maps.

Besides offering alternatives when things get sticky on your intended route, good maps will allow you to look ahead. If there's a tiny county road that looks promising, it's no hassle at all to check on its condition with some of the locals in the preceding town. And by actually laying out the thing in front of someone, their slow scan of those squiggly lines will often spark a suggestion for a route that you hadn't even considered.

"Ya want sceenry? Road 235 is sceeny! Wha, they took the guvnah himself down that road three years ago! Said he had his face agin the window the whole time. Beeeuutiful! You want sceenry? You'll pedal that contraption a long ways before you find anything fina than 235!"

There are basically five levels of planning maps that can be of use to the long-distance cyclist: national and international, state, county, national forest, and topo maps. Each is worth the cyclist's careful consideration.

National and international maps: These are obviously going to be some of the first maps you'll consult, the ones you pore over when you're supposed to be working or studying, but somehow can't seem to keep from daydreaming about all those points unknown. Any good library will have extensive collections of foreign and domestic atlases. If you want your own, start with Rand McNally for the U.S., and use Michelin Guides for Europe.

State maps: State maps are good for getting a slightly better feel for some of the attractions available in the regions you plan to traverse. Some are even complete enough to serve as your sole route guide, especially in sparsely populated areas. On the whole, the maps offered by the state departments of tourism are usually more complete than those offered by oil companies. They tend to be updated more often, allowing you to keep close track of new routes, as well as those no longer open for travel. Maps put out by state governments are also more likely to list recreational and camping sites, and highlights of pride-and-joy attractions (with photos) are usually plentiful on the flip side.

Unfortunately, many state maps don't spend much time investigating secondary routes, so those tempting blue and black lines can be anything from blacktop to gravel. If you choose to use only a state map, by all means check with locals on the condition of every off-the-beaten-

path route you plan on traveling. (In the forested areas of the western
United States, it's a good idea to get such feedback no matter how complete your maps. Secondary roads here are often heavily used by logging
trucks—beasts to be avoided at all costs.)

State maps are usually inexpensive or free when ordered from the
addresses listed in the Appendix. You can expect to wait several weeks
for a response, but sending along a self-addressed stamped envelope will
definitely help to grease the dragging gears of state government. An even
quicker alternative is to simply request a map by phone from the
chamber of commerce or tourist bureau in one of the state's more
populous cities.

County maps: If you plan on thoroughly exploring a relatively small
geographical area, county maps are hard to beat. They may not show
points of interest or camping areas, but you'd be hard pressed to get a
more complete and up-to-date picture of all available roads and how
they are surfaced. These are the true guides to what's left of backroad
cycling. Some county governments even classify their roads according to
average number of vehicles per day, something that can be a great help in
route planning. A traffic count of 500 to 1000 vehicles per day, for
instance, is quite tolerable, while 2500 will not leave you with much time
for enjoying the scenery.

County maps are relatively expensive: a price of $1.50 to $3 plus
shipping, is fairly common for a half-inch to one-inch-to-the-mile sheet.
And in the western United States, it's not uncommon for a county to be
divided into five or six sheets. At that rate, going halfway across the country can get rather expensive. Your best bet is to request an index to all the
counties, compare it with the information gleaned through the tactics offered in the following sections, and then order only those that seem particularly necessary or desirable. The United States Geological Survey also
has many county maps in topographic form, at about $3.25 each.

National forest maps: Though they aren't always up-to-date,
national forest maps nevertheless offer a wonderful overview of camping
and recreational areas, and, to a certain extent, physical land features
that the cyclist will undoubtedly find interesting. At approximately two
miles to the inch, forest maps are great for detail. You may go through
one every couple days or so if you ride a relatively straight line, but for a
more thorough exploration of a relatively small geographical area, they
are indeed ideal. As you finish with each forest, stick the map in an
envelope and mail it home. When ordered through one of the addresses
in the Appendix, count on spending at least a dollar apiece. Again, a self-
addressed stamped envelope will speed up the reply.

Topos: For the ultimate in being able to anticipate the land ahead, go with the topography maps put out by the U.S. Geological Survey. Maps of entire states (both in shaded relief and topographic contours) are commonly available in scales of 1:500,000 or 1:1,000,000. This translates into roughly eight and sixteen miles to the inch, respectively.

If you plan to do a great deal of hiking or exploring in a very small area, a scale of 1:24,000 (2000 feet to the inch) is fine. A scale of 1:100,000 (1.6 miles to the inch), however, should be more than ample for all but the fanatically curious. To cover an area 40-by-40 miles even at this scale, you'll be packing a sheet almost three-by-three feet—not exactly a back pocket bundle.

Your first step should be to write the USGS for complete indexes to the states you're interested in (see address in the Appendix). If you're short on space or funds, or both, concentrate your purchases on areas where a preview of the terrain would be especially helpful in making route decisions.

Do keep in mind that topo maps can be way out-of-date. Missing roads and buildings should be expected, requiring that you keep a sharp eye out for key drainages and land patterns when following remote dirt roads. Whenever you take a break in the middle of nowhere, it's great training to use land contours to determine your exact position.

If you use a compass, make sure you take into account the magnetic declination of the area, which is usually given at the bottom of a topo sheet. Stand well away from your bike when taking readings, so the metal mass doesn't turn north into south. An excellent discussion of map and compass techniques can be found in *The Wilderness Route Finder,* by Calvin Rutstrum.

Once you've gotten a decent collection of reference maps, the real fun of planning a bike trip begins. Basically, there are four considerations that go into choosing specific routes. These are: attractions and scenery, climate, road conditions, and, for some, availability of campgrounds or lodging. The purpose of looking into each of these points is not to eliminate the adventure of a trip, but rather to make sure that, on a limited schedule, you can experience the best an area has to offer. The following discussion is meant to help you route a trip that will be pleasant, exciting, and fun. How deeply you wish to dive into the research pool is entirely up to you.

ATTRACTIONS AND SCENERY

I'll assume that you have a general idea of the region you'd like to travel through (northern West Coast, Colorado Rockies, French wine country, castles of England, for instance). If your route will concentrate on areas in the United States and Canada, the most logical place to start assembling information is from the various state and provincial transportation and tourism departments (addresses listed in the Appendix). In letter form, detail your areas of interest as much as possible, being sure to relate your intentions to travel by bicycle. Explain whether you plan to camp or look for rustic inns. If you'd like to tour old Colorado mining towns located on the west slope of the Rockies, camping most of the time but staying in motels once a week, then that's precisely what you should put in your letter. More often than not, you'll receive a packet of information sufficient to at least start laying down routes.

For city-oriented information, request a list of chamber addresses from the state department of tourism, or look up their addresses in the *World Wide Chamber of Commerce Directory,* published by Johnson Publishing company of Loveland, Colorado. This neat little guide goes well beyond a healthy list of American chambers of commerce. There is also a guide to U.S. consulates and embassies in foreign countries, as well as foreign consular offices in the U.S. The guide can be found in larger libraries throughout the country. I should mention that over the last several years, many of the larger cities have begun calling their tourist agencies "visitor bureaus." They still have chambers of commerce, but these are now offices dealing strictly with regional business matters. Whether operating as chambers or visitor bureaus, these agencies will prove especially helpful in providing information on local history and recreation areas.

If you will be dealing with foreign tourism departments, you'll find it helpful to enclose with your request, a large self-addressed stamped envelope with a generous number of international reply coupons. These can be obtained from most U.S. post offices of any size, and each one is equivalent to one ounce of postage anywhere in the world. At 60 cents apiece they aren't exactly cheap, but they will often save you several weeks of waiting.

For all the great help that chambers and visitor bureaus can offer, the one problem with their information is that it is always generic in nature. No amount of pleading will get you the inside scoop on the best quiche in Flint, Michigan. And if you become struck with the quaint look of that Italian restaurant down the street, don't expect the chamber of commerce to be the one to tell you that the meatballs bounce when they're dropped. For this information, one must wander through the wilderness of "where-to-do-it" books, scanning hundreds of pages for the attractions and establishments with the biggest splattering of stars or checks or happy faces. Actually, such guides can be a real help when you're deciding where to spend that hard-earned money, though I must confess that I'm still confused as to just how much an extra grinning little face is really worth. For a quick peek into various attractions, go with Frommer's, Fodor's or Michelin. Then when you're ready to get more serious, dive into the American Express Pocket Guides, and the excellent British-produced Blue Guides.

ROAD CONDITIONS

Unless you plan to travel on an actual bicycle route, picking roads can be a rather formidable task. The number-one problem with choosing on hunch alone can be summed up in one word: shoulders. With adequate space to the right of that white line, speeding traffic and swaying RVs become much more tolerable. Without it, you must expect to bear the brunt of horns and curses, along with an occasional ill-timed move that may require taking to the ditch.

Of course, the less traffic a road has, the less important a shoulder becomes (which is fortunate, since backroads rarely have shoulders). Therefore, your strategy should be to stay on sparsely traveled roads, and when that becomes impossible, pick a "red highway" that has satisfactory shoulders. Either task can be something of a challenge.

From all those wonderful maps you've acquired, there will probably be no shortage of blue or black lines from which to choose. It's usually best to go ahead and route yourself and then contact the appropriate agencies and clubs for a second opinion.

To begin with, check any particularly questionable part of your route with the county highway department. Describe your route step-by-step, being sure to mention whether you'll be traveling through the county on a weekday or weekend. Because the agencies deal with repair requests and funding allocations, they can usually give you a good deal of insight into the condition and use of the roads you propose to travel. At the bare minimum they should be able to spot a real ringer. If you can spring for the phone bill, you'll find that, on a county level, calling works better than writing letters.

If there is a question regarding whether or not you will be allowed to ride on special access roads, such as interstates or major multi-lanes, you may find it easier to place a call to the state highway commission. Offices will be located in the state capital, as well as in larger towns throughout the state.

Other great sources of routing information are bike clubs and shops. They probably won't be familiar with every road in their area, but they too should at least know which ones to avoid. The best approach to most clubs is to simply tell them the points "A" and "B" of your ride through their area and get back in touch a week or so later. This allows them to collect the opinions of their members who have made similar rides in the past.

You should use clubs extensively when traveling through any major metropolitan area, even if you're following a published bike route. Conditions can change so quickly in urbania that some routes can become inappropriate, if only on a temporary basis, almost before the information you read hits print.

If it's at all possible to force yourself into doing it, keep a daily road journal. You'll get a terrific amount out of it if you can combine basic road information with descriptions of the scenery, people, and events encountered along the way. However, if you're not into such rambling prose, a very simple journal can be made merely by dividing your pages into specific columns. Some likely headings might be: road name and location, shoulder conditions, traffic, scenery, and recreational opportunities. At the end of the day, give each category a quality rating of one to five.

At first such records may seem like a waste, especially to those riders who rarely repeat routes. More often than you might think, though, you'll stumble across an opportunity in the future to weave particularly great stretches of past trips into other rides. And in addition to route info, it can also be nice to have a directory of particularly good restaurants and campgrounds you encountered the first time through. If you feel benevolent, most cycling clubs would appreciate having a copy of your log to pass on to other cyclists. After all, each of us has memories of certain stretches of roadway where it all seemed to come together for us (as well as stretches where "it" had never been further from reach!). Distance cyclists seem to thrive on war stories and route rambles; there's little doubt that your information will one day find a receptive ear.

7

Rain

Few people really *like* riding in the rain, though many are able to overlook it. How you choose to react will depend partially upon whether you can ignore the rush of water coursing down your hindquarters, as well as the fact that each drop of water is bent on ultimately doing horrible things to the moving parts of your bicycle. But beyond such annoyances, other considerations, such as temperature, visibility, road conditions, traffic, and lightning must be considered.

If you happen to be in a town or city when the sky lets loose, there will be plenty of places to run for cover. Gas stations with pump overhangs, post offices, libraries, restaurants with foyers or overhangs, park shelters, stores, and bus stations are just a few of civilization's finer rain shelter offerings.

Even if you don't mind riding in the rain, at least hole up for the first 15 or 20 minutes, especially if you happen to be in an urban area. During this initial period of rainfall, the water mixes with road oil and exhaust residue to form an extremely slick road surface. This is an especially significant hazard in arid cities, where streets are cleaned far less often. After a short wash-down, reasonable traction will be restored.

Keep in mind that the distance required to stop in wet weather with aluminum rims will be almost doubled, and with steel, you may as well drag your feet. Eliminate water build-up on the rims by occasionally squeegeeing them lightly with your brake pads, especially after riding through standing water.

If it rains for very long, potholes may become hidden beneath standing water, making it very easy to break spokes and bend rims. Hang it up if you happen to be on a road with narrow, pockmarked shoulders.

One of the greatest dangers of wet-weather riding is reduced visibility. Many people cringe when it comes to driving a car in the rain, and a tense, uncertain driver may not react properly to you. The risk is especially great in vacation areas, since many four-wheelers will be totally unfamiliar with the roads. The drivers are likely to be peering through the drops for road signs, restaurants, rest stops, and the like, often leaving you to a chance sighting. Even competent, conscientious motorists who know just where they're going will suffer reduced visibility in wet weather. If you choose to ride in both rain and traffic at the same time, stay alert because you will have taken on a significant increase in hazard levels.

Lightning adds another unhappy dimension to the innocent summer shower. As death from lightning strikes is not exactly unheard of, under no circumstances should you ride during an electrical storm. If you're out on a prairie with few or no trees, crouch low, preferably in a roadside ditch. In forested areas, seeking shelter beneath one among many trees is fairly safe, though you shouldn't choose the tallest tree in the group. If strong winds are blowing, however, stay away from dead snags. It's

sometimes worth asking if you can get in someone's vehicle, since automobiles are well insulated from the dangers of lightning strikes.

If you're riding out in the country when bad weather strikes, shelters may be hard to find. Look for bridges, abandoned buildings, cliff overhangs, and barns (ask permission first). Be especially careful in areas prone to flash flooding, such as parts of the American Southwest, Mexico, the Middle East, Australia, and southern Italy and Spain. Roads that are dangerous will usually be so marked. HEED THESE WARNINGS! Obviously, don't take refuge in gullies or ditches; retreat to the nearest high ground. If it's an electrical storm, you can do little but lie low on a knoll and enjoy the show. Flash flooding conditions rarely last more than 45 minutes.

A rainstorm during even mildly cold weather can spell disaster in the form of hypothermia for the cyclist. The evaporative cooling effect of the relative wind causes an extremely rapid chilling of the body that can actually pose a threat to life. Do everything possible to avoid riding under such conditions.

CLOTHING

How you decide to dress for wet-weather riding will ultimately come down to a matter of trial and error. The reason that there are so many methods of dress used by cyclists today isn't because only a select few have caught on to the "right" way of doing it. The fact is, there is no perfect solution. Cyclists tend to mix-and-match rain gear until they have narrowed down the negative effects to a level that they can live with. The trousseau that eventually works best for you will also be a matter of personal tolerance.

One of the most common methods of rain protection is to employ that old standby—the poncho. The main advantages are that they are cheap, versatile (you can also use them for tarps or ground cloths), and easy to put on and take off. Many cyclists complain about their lack of breathability, which means that even though you are protected from the rain, you can be soaked by inside condensation. Actually, the ventilation with ponchos is better than with a lot of other options. The fact is that some degree of inside condensation seems to occur to many riders no matter what kind of material they decide to go with. While getting damp is certainly annoying, you should remember that the moisture from inside condensation is at least relatively warm, which can help to reduce your chances of contracting hypothermia in cold, wet conditions. (For more about the effects of cold rain, see Chapter 10.)

One of the biggest drawbacks of ponchos is that they can flap around like a flag in a windstorm. Some riders fasten them over the handlebars with elastic, which minimizes flapping and covers the hands and front bag at the same time. Unfortunately, if there is any kind of wind accompanying the rain, this arrangement is like hoisting a sail—expect to put a lot of effort into fighting to stay on course. On mountain or coastal roads, where wind gusts can be more than a little formidable anyway, the practice can be downright dangerous.

You'll also have to accept the fact that ponchos let in a fair amount of water from underneath. Even with fenders, you can expect a rather wet lower half. The addition of inexpensive rain chaps to the ensemble is a good partial solution, especially since the opening at the rear will still allow the condensation that builds up in the legs to escape.

CLOTHING OPTIONS FOR
RAIN

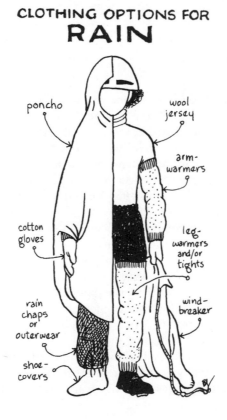

poncho

wool jersey

arm-warmers

cotton gloves

leg-warmers and/or tights

rain chaps or outerwear

wind-breaker

shoe-covers

A much more expensive alternative to the above set-up is to use Gore-Tex type outerwear, which repels water yet is designed to let body moisture escape. Before you go out and spend your paycheck, however, try to find someone who has an outfit that you could borrow for a wet-weather ride. Some people find that despite manufacturing claims, they still build up a fair sweat (though usually not anywhere close to the amount experienced in waterproof material). Other cyclists complain that while breathable materials work fine for the first few hours of a steady rain, they then seem to begin letting in more and more water. After several years of use, breathable fabrics can also begin leaking due to delamination of the materials. Finally, if you decide to purchase rain pants of this material, be sure to wear a pair of shorts on the outside of them, or your synthetic gold mine will quickly wear thin from the chafing of the saddle.

If you've managed to resign yourself to getting wet (but not cold), you may wish to consider buying a pair of good leg and arm warmers. The leg warmers are cheaper than tights, and you'll find them very useful on cold *dry* mornings, as well. A wool blend undershirt will keep your upper body warm, and one with long sleeves will in moderate weather eliminate the need for arm warmers. If you become chilled due to the relative wind, a nylon windbreaker will substantially reduce the effect of evaporative cooling. Once again, sewing mosquito netting under the arms, as recommended by Tim and Glenda Wilhelm in *The Bicycle Touring Book,* is well worth the effort because it allows the escape of body moisture.

Your feet are, unfortunately, destined to suffer the same wet fate as the rest of your body. Gore-Tex shoe covers are worthless without rain pants, as water will stream in at the tops. The best solution is probably to go with wool socks. Many people like wearing plastic bags inside their shoes, often building a layered effect consisting of a synthetic liner sock, the plastic bag, a thin wool sock, and finally the shoe. Indeed, your feet may become hot and sweaty, but as previously discussed, this is a reasonable alternative in a cold rain. Another option would be to wear a pair of dress rubbers over your shoes. As usual, don't expect them to keep your feet dry unless you wear chaps or high gaiters to keep water from entering at the tops. They will, however, help to reduce evaporative cooling.

Because wet, cold feet have a way of ruining an otherwise enjoyable evening, many cyclists opt for a spare pair of footwear for use around camp or "about town." The moccasins mentioned in Chapter 4, when covered with dress rubbers, offer a lightweight, compact alternative.

You may also want to wear a cheap pair of cotton gloves to keep your fingers warm in a cool rain. Waterproof construction worker's gloves will be even warmer, and the kind with rough palms will also help you keep a firm grip on the handlebars. And speaking of grip, cotton handlebar tape, as opposed to plastic, is much better for getting a good grip in wet weather.

People who wear glasses will have little choice but to endure a visual world of dancing drops, though these riders are at least spared the discomfort of having individual raindrops drive into their eyeballs. (Some riders actually prefer to wear sunglasses in the rain for this very advantage, though they run a certain danger from the lenses darkening an otherwise gloomy day to dangerous levels. A visor for the helmet would probably be a better solution.) If condensation from body heat builds up on the lenses of your glasses, try one of the liquid de-foggers available at most drug stores. Some of these liquids also seem to promote better runoff in a steady rain. If it gets to the point where water build-up is seriously distorting your vision, pull over and wait for things to moderate a bit. And if you've got contacts, wear them instead.

As a final word about clothing, make sure that you have a complete set of dry things to change into when the weather clears. Only if it is nice and warm should you opt for letting the breeze dry you out.

EQUIPMENT

No matter what the manufacturer may claim about his panniers, assume they will leak in the rain! Treating the seams of new panniers is of course recommended, but protection of your equipment from inclement weather should go much further.

To begin with, line each pannier with a *heavy duty* garbage bag (the 13-gallon size will do nicely). It's not a bad idea to then load clothes and delicate equipment into separate smaller bags, just in case the large one should get torn. Seal the large garbage bag with a twist tie (don't forget to take extras!), and tuck the neck down the inside of the pannier. A small but heavy bag to line your sleeping bag stuff sack is also advised. If you want, you can then place another waterproof stuff sack over the existing one, keeping the necks in opposite directions. The inside one makes a good pillow sack, and the double layer of material will provide protection from abrasion that could occur during a bad fall.

For intricate gear such as camera equipment, I use quality zipper-top bags and double bread sacks. Pretty sophisticated, I know, but then I don't often ride in the rain if I can help it. When it's unavoidable, this less than one ounce of protection is worth many dollars of cure. When weather is mild, bags can be left open for easy access. When your plastic bags wear thin or tear, as they certainly will, replace them immediately. River bags, such as those used by canoeists, are available for around $15 or $20 and will allow you to ride through a lake with little adverse effect.

When rain begins, check that all plastic bags and pannier and handlebar zippers are completely closed and that the protective zipper flap is turned down. With panniers that strap closed, be sure that the "neck" of the sealed garbage bag is pointing toward the rear wheel.

Regarding fenders, there is no clear-cut answer as to their necessity. If you know you will be doing a good deal of riding in wet climates, they're probably worth it. They will, after all, aid a bit in keeping muddy water off chain and rider. If you do not intend to ride in particularly wet climates, an occasional wet "skunk stripe" down your back seems to me better than the hassle of cleaning, straightening, and finagling fenders. (As mentioned in Chapter 4, such water spouts can be sharply reduced by placing a cut piece of foam padding over the rear rack before loading your equipment. The farther it extends over the rear wheel, the smaller will be your skunk stripe.)

CAMPING

Believe it or not, camping in the rain can be fairly tolerable. The two biggest areas of concern are keeping yourself, as well as all of your food, clothing, and delicate equipment dry, and repacking wet tents and tarps with as little water and real estate as possible. If it's pouring when you arrive in camp, you may want to rig the emergency shelter suggested under "Tarps and Ground Cloths" in Chapter 4 until a break occurs (assuming one does). This will allow you to study the wet terrain in order to determine the driest, least muddy spot in which to set up camp. It should go without saying that you ought to look for elevated grassy areas, as opposed to bare ground. Unfortunately, many public campgrounds will have grown bald long before your arrival. In such cases, look for the highest ground, well away from the runoff of concrete parking slabs or roadways. In desert areas, stay away from low spots, gullies, or washes.

If you've packed your shelter according to the "togetherness rule," you should be able to erect it even in a good rain without allowing the inside floor or walls to become soaked. To guard against the moisture that does end up on the floor, roll out your foam pads and transfer your panniers, sleeping bag, and handlebar bag to these pads. If things are considerably wet inside, as may happen in a driving rain, leave your bag rolled up until the moisture evaporates. It's unlikely that there will be enough moisture to hamper the warmth of your bag, but what soaks in may travel with you the next morning.

Try to manage all operations with feet outside, or shoes off. The amount of mud that can get tracked into a tent is unbelievable, and what doesn't dry in time will go with you. It's a good idea to carry an extra garbage bag with you as a doormat for wet and muddy shoes, clothes, and other paraphernalia.

Unless the wet weather has really chilled you, rainy evenings in camp are great for no-cook meals. (Several suggestions can be found in Chapter 15.) If you decide to go ahead and cook, it will have to be done under a separate shelter, or much more likely, inside the tent. Tents can be very flammable! In a matter of seconds, your entire assemblage of equipment (as well as yourself) could go up in smoke. If your tent has guy ropes angled from the peak of the door to the ground, you may want

to use a piece of plastic to form a simple A-frame shelter over it. Setting up the tent with the door adjacent to a tarp-covered picnic table is another alternative, though getting in and out :ๆn be like going through combat training.

If you absolutely must cook in the tent, do so as close to the unzippered door as possible. Have all seasonings, pots, and food laid out within *easy* reach. Place the stove on a fairly large piece of plastic or foam. This way, if the stove turns over and a fire starts, the entire blaze can be quickly shoved out the door. Be especially careful when firing up the stove, as some models can bellow out 18-inch-high flames before mellowing out to a reasonable cooking level. If a driving rain keeps you from operating your stove under such safety rules, don't use it!

If it's still raining the next morning, it's best to stay put. Packing a wet tent will add significant weight to your load. When the rain finally stops, completely pack your panniers inside the tent. Picnic tables will still be wet, and post-storm breezes are wonderful at blowing maps, handkerchiefs, and other light items into nearby mud puddles. Much of the water still clinging to the tent can be shaken off. If there are two of you, pull the tent taut from opposite ends and slap the sides with your hands. Clothes that are still wet will dry fairly quickly if strapped outside your packs with bungee cords. Just make sure there are no dangling strings or sleeves to get caught in the spokes. This practice is not necessarily a good idea if the roads are wet and you're not equipped with fenders. The other alternative is to place wet clothes on top of your closed garbage bag liners, and then zipper or strap the pannier shut about two-thirds of the way.

Anyone planning to ride and camp in climates known for wet weather should probably put a little more money into their shelter. When rain storms last for a week or more (not uncommon in some parts of the world), a tent can become a very valuable retreat for the cycle camper. Don't underestimate your psychological need for a dry, albeit tiny, place of refuge in a wet, wet world.

EQUIPMENT MAINTENANCE

Prolonged rains are not exactly a bike's best friend. The biggest problem is the washing away of lubricants from chains, cables, wheels, and derailleurs, and the splashing of mud and grit into exposed mechanisms. Even when not riding, always try to shelter your bike from rain. As I mentioned in Chapter 4, a small, rolled tarp with stretched guy lines and clips is handy for such protection.

There are certainly no set rules for lubrication in wet-weather riding, but the following can be used as a general guide.

Chain: After each rain, clean all grit from chain, cogs, and derailleur wheels with a cotton cloth. Use *only* the finer lightweight oils for lubricating such parts.

Derailleur: Clean and lubricate on bike after each rain. Remove, clean, and lubricate idler wheels every 24 hours of wet-weather riding.

Cogs: Clean and lubricate after each heavy rain.

Wheel greasing: Regrease after every five-to-seven days of wet riding.

Cables (brake and derailleur): Be sure all cables are greased *before* setting out. Then regrease after seven-to-ten days of wet riding.

Crank: Regrease after five-to-seven days of rain riding.

Shift levers: Lubricate with light oil after each rain.

RAIN FACTORING

There's a fairly simple technique the cyclist can employ to make a rough estimate of the influence that rain may have on a particular trip. The National Oceanic and Atmospheric Administration publishes a list of cities and their average number of days with precipitation for each month of the year (see table). October in Seattle, for instance, has an average of 13 rain days, or nearly one-half of the month. If a cyclist is determined not to ride in the rain at all, he would have to allow at least three or four layover periods for every week of Seattle-area riding. October in San Francisco, on the other hand, averages five days of rain, or roughly one-sixth of the month. Here, you could reasonably hope to keep layover days down to one or two a week.

This method is *not* meant to predict the actual number of rain days that will occur each week, or even where layovers will be required. Fronts come through in irregular patterns, and small geographical pockets can differ greatly from the nearby "averages." But the method can give the cyclist a *rough estimate* of the likely number of rain days for an entire trip.

Working out the figures for a four-week trip from Seattle to Los Angeles in October, using one week each of Seattle, Portland, San Francisco, and Los Angeles precipitation for the numbers, the cyclist can expect about eight days of wet weather. This figure should be used to help plan for the *likely number* of necessary motel nights and reduced mileage days. Of course, this technique should be supplemented by advice from local residents, where possible.

Who knows? You may end up with four solid weeks of rain. But if used in a generalized manner, "rain factoring" can help you play the odds a little better. The information gleaned from such tables might also convince you to change the timing of your trip to an earlier or later month.

Average Number of Days with Precipitation of at least .01 Inches
Selected Cities of the United States

City	January	April	July	October
Albuquerque, N. Mex.	4	3	9	5
Amarillo, Tex.	4	5	9	5
Anchorage, Ak.	7	7	11	12
Atlanta, Ga.	11	9	12	6
Baltimore, Md.	10	11	9	7
Birmingham, Ala.	12	9	13	6
Boise, Idaho	12	8	2	6
Boston, Mass.	12	11	9	9
Buffalo, N.Y.	20	14	10	11
Burns, Oreg.	13	7	3	6
Charleston, S.C.	10	7	14	6
Cheyenne, Wyo.	6	10	11	5
Chicago, Ill.	11	13	9	8
Cincinnati, Ohio	12	12	10	9
Cleveland, Ohio	16	14	10	11
Concord, N.H.	11	11	12	12
Dallas, Tex.	7	9	5	5
Denver, Colo.	6	9	9	5
Des Moines, Iowa	7	10	9	7
Detroit, Mich.	13	12	9	9
Duluth, Minn.	12	11	11	9
El Paso, Tex.	4	2	8	4
Eugene, Oreg.	18	12	2	11
Eureka, Calif.	16	12	2	9
Fairbanks, Ak.	7	5	12	10
Flagstaff, Ariz.	7	6	12	5
Grand Junction, Colo.	7	6	5	5
Hartford, Conn.	8	7	6	9
Helena, Mont.	9	8	7	6
Honolulu, Hawaii	10	9	8	9
Houston, Tex.	11	7	10	8

City	January	April	July	October
Indianapolis, Ind.	12	12	9	8
Jackson, Miss.	12	9	11	5
Juneau, Ak.	18	17	17	24
Knoxville, Tenn.	13	11	11	8
Las Vegas, Nev.	3	2	3	2
Lexington, Ky.	13	12	11	8
Little Rock, Ark.	10	10	9	6
Los Angeles, Calif.	6	4	*	2
Marquette, Mich.	17	11	10	12
Memphis, Tenn.	10	10	9	6
Miami, Fla.	7	6	14	11
Milwaukee, Wis.	11	12	10	9
Minneapolis, Minn.	9	10	10	8
Newark, N.J.	11	11	10	8
New Orleans, La.	10	7	15	5
New York, N.Y.	11	11	10	8
Norfolk, Va.	10	10	11	8
Oklahoma City, Okla.	5	8	7	6
Omaha, Nebr.	7	10	9	6
Peoria, Ill.	9	12	9	7
Philadelphia, Pa.	11	10	9	7
Phoenix, Ariz.	4	2	4	3
Pittsburgh, Pa.	15	13	11	10
Portland, Maine	11	12	9	9
Portland, Oreg.	19	14	4	13
Providence, R.I.	11	11	9	8
Raleigh, N.C.	10	9	11	7
Rapid City, S.Dak.	7	10	9	5
Saint Louis, Mo.	8	11	9	8
Salt Lake City, Utah	10	10	4	6
San Francisco, Calif.	11	6	1	5
Seattle, Wash.	19	14	5	13
Shreveport, La.	10	9	8	6
South Bend, Ind.	15	13	9	10
Spokane, Wash.	15	9	4	8
Syracuse, N.Y.	19	14	11	12
Tampa, Fla.	6	5	16	7
Topeka, Kans.	6	10	9	6
Washington, D.C.	11	10	10	7
Yakima, Wash.	10	4	2	5

* less than a half-day per month

8

Wind

No matter where your cycling happens to take you, it's unlikely that you'll ever meet a more formidable opponent than the wind. If you're not careful, several days of bucking it can blow your mind as much as it will your body. Though you'll never beat winds every time, a thorough understanding of how and why they occur, as well as their general regional tendencies, can at least put the odds in your favor.

It should be noted that winds can present far greater problems than just the ability to advance successfully against them. Coasts, cliffs, and mountains are settings for dangerously strong crosscurrents that can blow you right into traffic. And if you happen to compensate just as the surge dies off, you could find yourself returning to lower altitudes the hard way. Needless to say, all this makes for some real white-knuckled riding.

If wet weather from a low pressure system happens to soak you, the cool winds that often follow could set the scene for hypothermia. This is especially common in the high mountains, where local winds are more frequent than not, and cold rain is often the only kind offered. It's hard to think of a more dangerous location to gamble with hypothermia, especially since one of the first signs of the sickness is often a loss of coordination.

AVOIDING PROBLEMS

Understanding why the wind blows as it does will sometimes allow you the infinitely preferable option of working with it, rather than against it. Like most functions of weather, however, the wind will hardly follow a prescribed pattern every time. You will find that "logical" wind patterns are only slightly easier to ride against than "illogical" ones. Both require patience, endurance, and a comfortable familiarity with the low end of that turned down handlebar.

For any long trip, knowledge of the prevailing wind patterns should be considered a necessity. Though some people seem to ride across entire continents with no thought to such things, I can't imagine taking such chances with a trip that has been months in the making. The prevailing North American summer winds run from west to east. All rides across the continent should respect this tendency. I've met more than one west-bound cyclist who finally had to hitch or ship his bike across the plains after seven to ten days of struggling against westerlies for a 15- to 20-mile daily advance.

Topography and composition of the earth's surface will set up fairly regular, though often reversible, wind patterns. Along coastal regions or large lakes, the adjacent land surface will heat up much more rapidly during the day than the surface of the water, causing inland air movement. At night the land cools off more rapidly, causing offshore breezes to occur. This latter effect, however, is less pronounced. Should you wish to avoid all cross winds along such areas, early-morning or late-evening riding would be advised.

Prevailing winds can also be predicted in many mountain valleys. The sun will tend to warm the air adjacent to a mountain slope more

PREVAILING WINDS: LAKESHORE

INSHORE   OFFSHORE
A.M.   P.M.

rapidly than the open parts of the atmosphere. This lighter air then begins to rush up the slope, carrying moist warm air up and out of the valley. At night, the air adjacent to the mountain will cool rapidly, causing a rush of the heavier cold air back into the lowlands. Both of these currents will tend to flow along the slopes, always in the direction of the valley. Thus, you can expect a good tailwind climbing toward the high peaks in the morning, as well as when descending to their bases late in the evening.

The scenario may be somewhat complicated during the day, however, when complex cross-wind patterns flow laterally out of the valley, to return again at night. Near glaciers such as you might encounter in Alaska or parts of Canada, sharp downdrafts will occur as soon as the valley air begins to warm, making a midday climb out of the "trough" a miserable affair. Just remember that all such air-mass movement is dependent upon the warming effects of the sun. If you can't make these tendencies work for you, then early morning and late evening will be the most suitable times to ride.

Don't forget that wind effects from irregular heating and cooling can occur *in addition* to prevailing winds, which is why wind charts may have regions where arrows point in more than one direction. The intensity of prevailing winds can increase in areas with no real topographical variations to deflect air currents, such as in the Plains States of America. It should be noted that collisions of warm and cold air masses occur frequently in such flat areas on a hot spring or summer day, resulting in extremely violent winds.

PREVAILING WINDS: MOUNTAIN

UPHILL

DOWNHILL

A.M.

P.M.

DRAFTING

If you happen to be traveling with at least one other person, you'll have a valuable trick up your sleeve: drafting. This is simply the practice of riding close together in a single line, so that the lead cyclist breaks the headwind for those that follow. Though many people seem to discount the effectiveness of drafting, I can think of no more important weapon in the battle of the blow. Granted, it must be done properly if you are to notice a significant difference, and it is not a technique for the timid or unstable rider.

Distances between riders should not extend beyond 18 inches—a fact that makes it advisable to ride with fingers poised near the brake levers at all times. The lead rider has a responsibility to keep a fairly straight course, prefacing all swerves and braking with the proper warning. Obviously, a road riddled with potholes or glass would not be suitable for this kind of cycling. Although there is considerably less effort being expended by the trailing rider, this position is significantly more difficult if you've never drafted before or are doing so with a new partner. The fixed gaze on the leader's rear wheel can be absolutely hypnotic, turning an unannounced swerve to miss a pothole into disaster.

After you've ridden in a draft line for awhile, you'll be able to judge the distance between your bike and the one in front of you without having to keep a constant watch on your front wheel. This will come only after miles of finessed riding, however, so keep your distance at about two feet at first, with concentrated advances when conditions allow.

Don't stay in the lead until you're about to collapse. It's far more effective to trade off fairly often, since too much fatigue will dangerously lengthen your reaction time.

In cross-wind conditions, the most effective following position may be slightly overlapping the leader's rear wheel. Be very alert for loss of control by the leader when cycling along coastal or mountain cliffs.

Advance warning of potholes is essential if you plan to continue riding on round wheels. Glass is not often seen until the last minute, so anticipate slowdowns while tires are cleaned with a gloved hand. Drafting is obviously not the way to ride for maximum enjoyment of the scenery, but it is definitely a technique worth practicing, and practicing some more. I promise you, it will often be the deciding factor as to who comes out on top at the end of the day — you, or the wind.

CAMPING

Although it's true that local winds often die down in the evening, this is certainly not always the case. In many areas, such as along coasts

or at high altitudes, the wind direction merely reverses. A knowledge of these local weather patterns can prove useful when it comes time to make camp. This is especially true for the tarp camper, whose bedroom can be easily invaded by a driving rain. During strong winds, merely attaching tarp clips to the shelter and fastening guy lines to a nearby tree will be inadequate. Such conditions call for running a separate support line underneath the apex of the tarp. It's also not a bad idea to roll one of the edges of the shelter around an additional taut line, assuming suitable tie-off points are available. Ideally, the bottom of the tarp is then staked with tarp clips or anchored at the corners with rocks. (Even no-stake tents should have a corner staking option available for high-wind situations. Just don't forget to take the stakes!)

A solid grove of trees is often the best protection from the wind, but make sure there are no tall dead snags or limbs that could thunder down on your camp.

Cooking can be a very trying experience in high winds. Besides having to cook on an irregular stove flame, you'll have to eat food well seasoned with dirt and sand. It's better to build a simple stone shelter with large rocks than to attempt to fire up in the tent. All in all, if you're not too chilled from the big blow, a cold meal is much easier to manage.

MAINTENANCE

The real danger that strong winds bring to your bicycle is to load the chain, derailleurs, and cogs with dirt and grit. This problem can be especially bad when riding past farm fields that have just been planted or along ocean beaches. Ideally, you should try to wait out such conditions, since riding in strong gusts is often just this side of fruitless anyway. If you must press on, be aware that your bike's exposed moving parts will suffer. As a temporary remedy, the chain, cogs, and derailleur can be wiped with a cotton cloth and then relubricated with light oil. Of course, there's no way you can get inside all the little nooks and crannies of these parts. Schedule a stop at a bike shop for a thorough cleaning, and expect to wait *at least* half a day for the completion of the task.

One wind-related problem for those riding in the American Southwest deserves special attention: dust storms. These are far from infrequent, and until you've gone through one, you have no idea of their severity. Though winds may increase steadily before the dust storm actually occurs, there is very little warning before visibility is reduced to zero. Should you be unfortunate enough to encounter such a storm, get as far off the road as possible. (And I mean way off! Climb any fences that get in your way.) This is important since automobile pileups are frequent under such conditions, with people commonly running up and down the ditches, into telephone poles, and other places besides the road. If you can get into a vehicle with someone without endangering your life, do so. Otherwise, cover your eyes, nose, and mouth with clothing, kneel down with your face against your lap, and wait it out. Within 15 or 20 minutes, things should be back to normal—everything but your bike, that is.

It's a mistake to ride the thing even 100 yards after it goes through such a storm. Damage will surely result. Hitchhike to a bike shop, and get used to the idea of sightseeing by foot for a couple of days. Such a repair bill is going to set you back a bit—no doubt about it. But if your bike is worth more than the cost to fix it, you really have no other alternative but to swallow hard and fork over the money. Whenever you enter a bike shop with a problem of this size, be sure to get an estimate for the work first. If you're lucky enough to be in a town with several shops, get more than one estimate.

Should you find yourself uncertain as to which of several shops to go with, take a look around and see what kind of equipment they sell. A place dealing in European 700C tires and Colnago frames may know more about what ails your touring machine than one loaded with nothing but economy bikes. Sometimes, the patrons themselves can offer clues to the shop. A number of "cyclish" looking people arguing over brazing techniques and gear clusters, for example, might at least offer a sign of competence, if not economy. Walls covered with club touring announcements and racing schedules are other things to keep an eye out for.

If you're stranded in a large town, first call a couple of shops and find out if there's a touring club in the area. (Try to avoid getting a club that is sponsored by that store.) Then give one of the members a holler and ask which shop tends to do the best work for the money. If the shop knows this person, ask him if you can drop his name when you take in the bike.

Remember, such dust-spawned hassles can usually be avoided. Most desert highways are lined with special warning signals to alert you to possible danger. If you encounter such a warning, get out of the area and into a shelter as soon as possible! Checking ahead with local weather stations and state police each day of your desert crossing is the surest way to avoid dust storms. With the possible exception of tornados or hurricanes, I can think of no condition under which bicycling seems more ill-advised.

PSYCHOLOGY

Do absolutely everything possible to become familiar with the wind's patterns in the region where you plan to ride. Though the wind may be an infrequent intruder where you live, there are geographical pockets where the breeze rarely dips *below* 10 to 13 miles per hour, with 20 to 25 miles per hour being common. Riding against such conditions will bring you misery beyond belief and will very likely force a major rerouting.

Unfortunately, even the most careful planning around local wind patterns provides no guarantee against substantial head winds. On such days, immediately reduce your anticipated mileage by one-third to one-half. Knowing that you don't have to achieve 70 miles by sundown will allow you to make the best of a bad situation. Stay in low gears, rest often, and draft whenever possible. If the headwinds persist for two or three days, it's a good idea to call the local weather station. Perhaps you've entered a very localized wind pattern that didn't show up on the charts. Or it could be as baffling to the forecasters as it is to you. Either way, they will probably be able to tell you the conditions farther along your route. If things look just as bleak ahead, you can either plug away and hope for the best or take advantage of the weird blow by rerouting, perhaps returning to your original route at a later date.

9

Heat

Heat is probably the most misunderstood of all the elements the cyclist will encounter, and therefore often the most underestimated. While we've all heard terrible tales of the sweltering Southwest deserts, the ill effects of the sun can debilitate an unprepared rider just about anywhere in the world. The most common problem relative to heat exposure is sunburn. In fact, each year a surprising number of cyclists are admitted to hospitals for the treatment of severe sunburn. And since a fair amount of time is necessary for convalescence, you can figure that your trip will usually end there.

It comes as a surprise to some to learn that the mountains are common backdrops for scores of severe sunburn cases. Riding shirtless past those refreshing summer snowfields may seem like a real kick, but on a 10,000-foot pass, your body may be receiving five times more ultraviolet waves from the sun than it does at sea level. In a surprisingly short amount of time, you can come out looking like a Rip Van Winkle who fell asleep under a heat lamp.

In addition to sunburn, there are two other heat-related maladies that the cyclist must be aware of: heat exhaustion and heat stroke. Very simply, heat exhaustion is a condition resulting from fluids being lost at a faster rate than they are being replaced. The first effects will leave you feeling as you might during the onset of a major bout with the flu. If you continue to lose fluids at such a rate, you could feasibly go into shock or heat stroke, or both. Be especially aware of the potential for heat exhaustion when riding in arid climates, since your body will tend to lose moisture from increased perspiration evaporation. Certain desert en-

vironments can be double trouble, since fluids are not available for great distances. Moral: Be prepared.

Heat stroke is a more severe problem than heat exhaustion, and results from a high internal body temperature. (While heat stroke *can* result from heat exhaustion, dehydration is not always a factor.) At a certain point during the onset of heat stroke, your body will actually stop trying to lower its temperature through perspiration. This can very rapidly lead to loss of consciousness and death. There are various danger signs, including loss of clear thinking and vision, an extremely hot feeling, and shortness of breath.

While hot, arid country is usually thought of as the most likely backdrop for such trouble, high humidity regions such as the southeastern United States can actually be more dangerous. The body's prime means of reducing its temperature is through evaporative cooling, caused when perspiration is constantly absorbed by the surrounding air. But on a hot Georgia day with 90 percent humidity, the air is too saturated to absorb much of what you perspire. Consequently, your body attempts to cool itself by diverting blood flow to your skin, which substantially reduces the amount available to other parts of the body. At the very least, and well before the actual onset of heat stroke, your ability to function in an aerobically efficient manner will be significantly reduced.

AVOIDING PROBLEMS

Since heat-related maladies tend to advance in severity very rapidly, prevention is the most sensible approach. As far as clothing is concerned, in general, you'll want to wear light-colored garments, a visor (preferably with a dark underside to reduce reflected glare), sunglasses, and a handkerchief or upturned shirt collar for neck protection. At this point, the debate regarding hot-weather clothing begins in earnest.

Actually, the particular combination of protection you select will depend greatly on where you plan to be riding. For instance, if you're planning to be in hot, arid regions (unavoidable if you're crossing the United States during the summer), opt for long-sleeved, medium-weight cotton shirts to retain a bit of body moisture while keeping sun out. A

CLOTHING OPTIONS FOR
HEAT

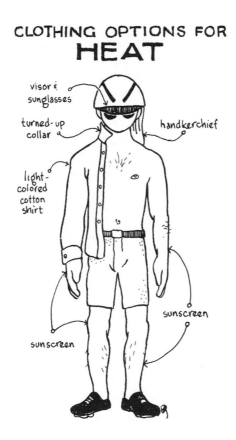

visor & sunglasses

turned-up collar

handkerchief

light-colored cotton shirt

sunscreen

sunscreen

pair of lightweight long pants will further increase your ability to retain moisture in arid climates, but I find them too restrictive to be worth the bother. Be sure to use a good sunscreen with a high sun protection factor on *all* exposed skin.

Other useful tricks to help you keep cool in arid regions include soaking your hat in water at every opportunity, and draping a wet hand towel over your head and shoulders, secured by your hat or helmet. You may look like you should be riding a camel instead of a bike, but at least for awhile, you'll be comfortable. You can also dig your damp washcloth out of its plastic bag for a bit of quick relief. Women will find a wet bandana stuffed into their bra to be a great, if somewhat unconventional, cooling system. If you plan to be riding in moderate- or high-humidity areas, forego the long-sleeved shirts for short-sleeved ones—again, preferably of cotton or cotton- polyester (but replace those long sleeves with sunscreen!).

With moderate levels of riding in high heat situations, you should plan on drinking a minimum of one gallon of water per day. While you may dislike the powdered electrolyte replacement drinks (especially if mixed full strength), they nevertheless replace a host of vital minerals lost through perspiration. Don't try to carry all of your liquids inside you —they weigh just as much, and you'll find that your stomach makes a lousy bota bag. Instead, sip small amounts of fluids throughout the day.

If your route will take you into the wide-open spaces, water stops can be a problem (50 to 75 miles between spigots is not uncommon). Water weighs in at over eight pounds to the gallon, but in this case, to heck with the weight. Don't *ever* take chances. Certain types of juice now comes in square, one-quart containers complete with handles. These make great additional water carriers to add to your cycling bottles, as they allow you to distribute the weight evenly on the bicycle, are easily crammed into a pannier or tied to something, and are simple to drink from while riding. Don't bother with so called "insulated" water bottles because the amount of liquid you can carry per container is substantially reduced, and you'll still have lukewarm toddy by 10 A.M. Anytime water is scarce, fill up whenever you can—even if all your containers are seven-eighths full. Of course you should never blindly drink from any open water you may come across, but such water can often be used to cool off your skin. (One warning here: Don't just jump into a deep body of water after riding—severe leg cramps can result.)

Another important consideration when riding in high heat situations is what and how much to eat. You shouldn't skip regular morning and evening meals, but don't gorge yourself at one sitting and expect it to meet your body's nutritional needs. This is an especially bad practice in hot weather and can easily lead to a hearty case of nausea. It's far better to eat small amounts throughout the day.

Juicy fruits, such as grapes, oranges, and grapefruits are great for such munchtimes since their high water-content helps to maintain body fluid levels. A mixture of nuts, granola, roasted soybeans, sunflower seeds, and the like also makes a great road snack. During hot-weather riding especially, I occasionally prefer to obtain my protein from such "gorp" rather than always taking it in the large doses found in meat. For one thing, meat takes a lot longer to digest, and it can actually speed up your metabolism enough to make the heat seem even more unbearable. I also try to avoid alcohol on hot days, since it promotes dehydration.

Though it's indeed important to maintain adequate salt levels, don't just pop salt tablets as if they were candy. Too much salt in concentrated form can do nasty things to your stomach. Recently, there's been some evidence to suggest that it's primarily potassium and magnesium, rather than sodium, that is lost through sweating. If this is indeed true, you'd do well to reach for fresh fruits and vegetables on a hot day. Salt does seem to help some people in the prevention of cramps, but before going to tablets, you may wish to try using a heavier hand with the salt shaker during meals.

Undoubtedly, many people think it better to cross regions of intense summer heat during the winter. Remember, though, that strong winds and occasional downpours are much more prevalent from December through March. If you do intend to traverse hot regions during the summer months, the only way to live with the heat is to hole up during the hottest part of the day (12 to 5 P.M.). Consider that if you leave at first summer light, you can often get 50 miles in by 11 A.M. Then write letters or journal entries, take photos, sleep, or get a guest pass at the local Y and shower. This is especially wise in the desert, since winds are usually strongest in the early to mid-afternoon hours. As evening approaches, the breezes will taper off again, allowing you a fairly pleasant ride to your final destination.

There is another, seldom-mentioned reason for holing up during the hottest part of the day, especially in the deserts of Arizona, Nevada, California, and northwestern New Mexico. More than once in these areas, I've encountered poorly laid asphalt that becomes soft under the intense afternoon sun. While this is certainly not a serious condition on most roads, the possibility for real problems shouldn't be ignored. Unfortunately, the only other people who are likely to know of such local conditions are other cyclists. It wouldn't hurt to call a few bike shops near these areas and see if they know of any such sticky riding along your proposed route.

One of the great advantages of cycle touring is the flexibility that it allows you. Some days you feel so great when you reach your intended destination that you pedal right on past it to an alternative one, 30 miles farther down the road. Regions of high heat, however, are not good places to exercise this option. I heartily recommend that you plan your "hole-ups" and stopover points regularly and stick to them. This is especially important in the "wide-open spaces," since jumping destination points may eventually leave you with a very long day under lousy riding conditions — the perfect setup for dangerous overexertion. Even in more populated areas, stay on schedule, or reduce it if you feel you're overdoing it. Unless you frequently ride in very hot conditions, your body just won't function as well as it does under more optimum temperatures.

CAMPING

After a long day of hot-weather riding, a comfortable night can be an important factor in keeping your spirits up. Some cyclists end up using their "rainy day" motel room allotment in very hot weather instead. Actually, you'll probably appreciate getting a room more when you're soaked to the bone and shivering than when you're wiped out from the heat. But the one fantastic thing that lures so many to the neon vacancy signs is a shower.

This wonderful invention, however, need not cost you the price of a room. Many state parks and recreation areas will have them, and even if they don't, a water spigot can do almost as nice a job. Just take your cooking pot over to one and proceed to cool down, one glorious pot after another. If you're in arid country, keep your cycling shorts on for the dousing — they'll dry on a line very quickly. In more humid regions, plan on taking a bathing suit or a pair of nylon running shorts. If you do decide to try a spigot shower, don't soap up at the faucets themselves, as other campers may get understandably upset by this. Instead, do your heavy-duty cleaning in the rest room. The same goes for rivers and lakes; don't wash in the body of water itself or on the shoreline. It may not be a pure mountain stream to begin with, but the sight of your soap bubbles drifting by — biodegradable or not — tends to make it seem all the worse. Before leaving in the morning, remember to dampen your washcloth and pack it away in a plastic bag. It will make a nice cool compress after a couple of hours on the road.

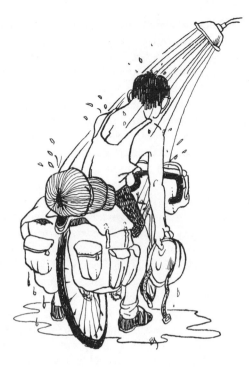

If you're lucky enough to have several camping areas to choose from, or decide to spend the night on public desert land, give some serious thought to where you'll unroll your bed. Desert or swamp, sleeping downwind from water can do a lot to keep you cool. (Without a tent, though, the mosquito factor may greatly outweigh the benefits.) When it's really hot, try to find a spot that is under constant shade. If you get in toward sunset and can't find any fully shaded areas, try to camp on the west side of a large object—a hill, mountain, or building. That way, you'll be spared those first hot rays of the morning sun. If you stop for the day in early or mid-afternoon, you'd be better off sleeping on the east or northeast side, and starting to ride again just as the sun tops the horizon the next morning.

No matter where you sack out, you'll probably find your sleeping bag much too warm for sleeping in regions of high heat. Covering up with a cotton sleeping bag liner is the perfect solution and will also help keep your bag clean.

When in the desert, there are definitely certain places where you should never camp. These include gullies, arroyos, washes, or ditches. Mountain rainstorms that you are not even aware of can send 4- to 6-foot walls of water down ravines in a lot less time than it would take you to get yourself and your equipment to high ground. Every year there are people killed by such flash floods, and to give you an idea of how strong the flow can be, many of them are washed away with their cars.

When you are randomly camping out on public lands, water, of course, will probably be nonexistent. Don't use all of your available supply, as serious need for it could develop during the next morning's ride— even if it's only a short hop to the next spigot. In these circumstances, premoistened towelettes are ideal for personal cleaning, and washing dishes with sand can work surprisingly well.

For obvious reasons, a stake-down tent is not always ideal for desert camping. With a little jury-rigging, however, it can be used fairly successfully, especially since summer nights in the desert are usually free from strong winds. Take extra long lines with you to tie ends and pullouts to nearby creosote or mesquite bushes, or to cacti (very carefully, I might add, for your sake, as well as the plant's). Rocks can be set on the inside corners to anchor the shelter.

It will take lots of care and plastic bags to keep sand out of your equipment, and even then, a daily shaking out should be anticipated. And, speaking of shaking, in most warm climates, clothing or shoes that have been lying on the open ground should be checked before they are put on again. You may just find a scorpion or black widow napping in them. Yes, there are some unpopular critters in the warmer climates, but a little common sense and precaution will keep you from ever developing an intense relationship with them.

EQUIPMENT MAINTENANCE

Riding in high temperatures is generally not hazardous to the health of your bike or equipment, but there are a few special things to watch out for. Don't fill your tires to maximum pressure early in the morning. The desert may kick off the day at 80 degrees, but 110 to 115 is just around the corner. (Add to that the fact that dark road surfaces may be 20 to 30 degrees hotter yet!) If you do want to start out at full pressure, be sure to put a gauge on your tires every hour or so, at least until the temperature peaks.

A hot, arid region will tend to dry out chain lubricants faster than normal. Have a can of lubricant ready just in case. Add a little wind to the scenario, and you can end up with a drive train full of sand and grit. If this happens, by all means get things cleaned and relubricated at first chance. As mentioned in Chapter 8, if your bike goes through a full-blown dust or sand storm, don't ride it another mile. Hitchhike to the nearest shop for a complete cleaning, repacking, and oiling.

There's one final thing to be aware of if you plan to ride in hot, humid conditions: gloves. If yours are starting to fall apart when you take off, a few days of hot, sweaty riding will probably finish them off. If you value their usefulness, as well you should, have the old ones bronzed and buy a new pair before leaving.

MEDICAL TREATMENT

There's nothing wrong with being a little extra paranoid about riding in intense heat. But when, for whatever reason, things do go wrong under the blistering sun, here's what to do about it.

Sunburn: A mild sunburn may be treated by simply applying liberal amounts of sunscreen lotion to the affected areas to prevent drying. If you happen to be in the desert, the juice of the relatively common aloe vera plant can be quite soothing on mild cases. Of course, all affected areas should be covered from any further exposure to the sun. If the case is severe enough to result in blistering of the skin, avoid the use of oils or lotions, as these may contribute to the spread of infection. Instead, apply cool sterile dressings to relieve pain.

Aspirin may help fight the discomfort, but you can expect some miserable days and nights ahead. If you decide to continue riding, dressings will have to remain on the blistered areas to avoid infection, and if you've really overdone it, swelling may make any further riding impossible.

Heat exhaustion: The symptoms of heat exhaustion are nausea, rapid heartbeat, pale facial color, and sweaty, but cold and clammy skin. Treatment is relatively simple. Have the victim lie in the shade with feet slightly elevated. Loosen any restrictive clothing, and administer sips of cool liquids as long as he is conscious. Recovery should occur spontaneously. After the victim has rested in this position for a good 45 minutes, replenish salt and water loss.

High energy foods, such as chocolate, nuts, and granola are good at this point. If it's still extremely hot, just stay put until later in the day. When you do leave, try to transfer some of the victim's load into your panniers.

Remember, heat exhaustion can occur to someone who is in very good shape. It's always a good idea to train in hot weather if part of your trip will require traveling in it. This will help your body's cooling system—the sweat glands and blood vessels—to more easily adapt to similar conditions on the road.

Heat stroke: Heat stroke is an extremely serious condition, with death too often being the final result. Symptoms may include poor coordination, an extremely hot feeling (or in a few cases, a cold feeling), and deliriousness. Unlike heat exhaustion, where the face is pale, heat stroke victims will have a flushed face and, as a rule, dry skin. Doctors aren't quite sure why heat stroke occurs, but it seems to happen more frequently when there has been no relief from sweating over the past 24 hours. Remember this when considering plugging on through the desert day and then spending an 85-degree night among the cacti.

To treat heat stroke, you must first cool the victim's body down as soon as possible. Ice packs, immersion in a stream or lake, covering with a wet cloth, and fanning are all methods to achieve this. (This is another reason why bottles should always be full when riding in the desert.) Massage arms and legs in an effort to achieve blood flow in the extremities. This will help to cool down internal organs.

When the victim appears to be out of pain and is alert, stop treatment. You can actually lower temperature too fast. Make a grandstand effort to flag down a passing motorist and get the injured person to a hospital as quickly as possible. *Never* continue riding, no matter how good things may look, as the person will very likely have an intolerance for heat for quite some time after recovery. Don't forget: Heat stroke is *not* merely an advanced stage of heat exhaustion, so there will be no such warnings. Stopping often to cool down on a very hot ride may seem like a hassle, but it could save your life.

10

Cold

There are certainly times when riding in relatively cold weather is preferable to a summer fry on the blacktop. Appetites are sharp, hills seem more tolerable, muscles less reluctant. But cold weather does harbor a rather impressive fleet of caveats which, if ignored, can rapidly lead to sickness or injury. Besides frostbite, there's old familiar hypothermia, a condition which frequently occurs in wet weather in the 35- to 50-degree range. Such temperatures are not at all infrequent at high altitudes even in summer, though spring and fall are the seasons most likely to cause problems. Without adequate clothing, you have no business traveling under such conditions.

When the mercury drops below 32 degrees, a whole new weather scenario can be rapidly introduced in the form of ice and snow. Of course, such things reduce your traction and the traction of passing motorists to almost nothing. Ice particles can build up on rims, potholes become hidden beneath the fluff, and road salt or sand quickly moves in on your bike's moving parts. Though it's unlikely that anyone would purposely ride a fully loaded bicycle through such conditions, it happens, especially on the high side of a mountain. If you get caught in the flakes, consider two points before slushing onward: (1) Are you in immediate danger from passing traffic or unguarded mountainsides? (2) Are conditions right for hypothermia (chilled wet skin and a good breeze)?

Even if the answer to either question is "maybe," can the whole affair! If you're above timberline, not only will conditions be at their worst, but it's unlikely that there will be many appropriate places of

refuge. Standing well off the roadway itself, at a turnout or wide stretch of shoulder, stick out your thumb and catch a ride. People are extremely willing to help under such conditions. If you're into the challenge, but not the loss of life, have them just take you to the protection offered below timberline. Set up camp, remove any wet clothes, and retire to the womb of your sleeping bag. Hot liquids and foods are a good idea if you can prepare them out of the weather.

As in any extreme weather, cold-weather riding is closer to the edge of danger. By necessity, this type of travel turns into a thinking person's game, centered around a constant consideration of "what if." If you care to play, be sure to learn the set of rules that follows.

CLOTHING

For obvious reasons, clothing should be the number one consideration for any type of cold-weather riding. The combinations open to you are indeed vast, though I tend to narrow down the choices as the severity of the weather increases. For a relatively mild chill in the air, wool jerseys and leg warmers will be sufficient. Synthetic-wool blends will certainly cost less, but their usefulness will bottom out at a temperature significantly above pure sheep. Wool absorbs perspiration, and then releases it at a gradual rate. This allows your body to maintain a more constant temperature.

You are quickly entering the danger zone if your clothing begins to feel wet, since evaporative cooling can induce hypothermia in no time at all. Always change wet clothing!! Of course the situation becomes serious if you happen to be riding in a cold rain. Although pure wool will still insulate you, the evaporative cooling effect on wet material can reduce its warming properties enough to pose real danger. Your best choice is a Gore-Tex or similar outer covering, which will protect you from wind while maintaining its breathability.

In cold, dry weather, a down vest is good for keeping the vital organs warm, and it is compact and light enough to not cause the problems with packing that sweaters and jackets do. Add a light windbreaker to help reduce the cooling effects of cold breezes. Since circulation to the hands is sometimes restricted when riding, down gloves or mittens (if you can brake with them) are not a bad idea. Polarguard or heavy wool, though bulkier, will of course be much more effective in wet weather.

CLOTHING OPTIONS FOR
COLD

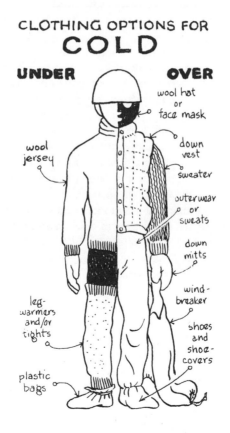

UNDER

wool jersey

leg-warmers and/or tights

plastic bags

OVER

wool hat or face mask

down vest

sweater

outerwear or sweats

down mitts

wind-breaker

shoes and shoe-covers

A hat is an extremely important item of clothing, since as much as 80 percent of the body's heat can be lost through the head. Thin wool caps and ski masks are always good choices, as is a silk scarf wrapped around the head and ears, secured by your helmet. Thin wool ski caps and headbands will also fit under a helmet without any problem.

As for feet, wool is again a good solution. Gore-Tex shoe covers are an expensive, rather imperfect invention, yet they do keep inside condensation to a minimum. A much cheaper solution would be to adopt the plastic bag layering technique discussed in Chapter 7. Your feet will get very wet from sweating, but they will at least be warm. For maximum protection, start with a silk liner sock, followed by a plastic bag, then a thicker wool sock. If there's room in the shoe, go ahead and put another plastic bag on the outside of this last sock. Be careful, however, that the shoe is not then fitting so tightly that it restricts circulation. Standard cycling shoes offer no insulation whatsoever in cold weather, and many don't have enough "give" to layer up with good socks. Don't set out to tour cold climates with these until you've tested them out on short trips in the cold.

One other thing: Cycling, of course, induces relative wind. At 15 miles per hour in calm but bitter cold conditions, flesh can freeze in minutes. Be especially careful to protect your nose, ears, and cheeks. Also be aware that metal glasses can freeze to your face, as can tools and certain metal parts to your exposed fingers. Be sure you have along a thin pair of gloves to handle repairs. Even in warmer weather, the effects of wind can chill a cyclist to a dangerous level. When making mountain descents, you will routinely be coasting in cool air for as long as 20 to 30 minutes at a time. This sudden change from a sweaty climb to the top can be bad news to your body. Always keep a windbreaker handy and slip into it at the summit—not halfway down after you're already chilled!

Reduce your expected mileages in cold weather. It's hardly worth getting frostbitten to make the "mileage grade." Besides, you'll probably find that the additional bulk of wearing more clothing will add significantly to your wind resistance.

RIDING TECHNIQUE

If the road becomes snow covered, use your brakes to squeeze the moisture from your rims, as you would during a rain. This will also keep ice from forming on the brake pads. Should you feel yourself going into a skid, steer into it, as you would in a car, and have your legs ready for support. If you're riding with cleats, a slight loosening of the toe straps will allow you to pull free very quickly should the need arise.

Be especially cautious of frozen streams of ice across mountain roads, where snow melts during the afternoon, then becomes frozen again during the night. Also, passing automobiles will glaze many an intersection or hill.

Riding on snow or ice is at best a very poor gamble; sooner or later you're going to go down. The only way that you should find yourself riding in such conditions is by accident. If it's a localized condition, such as might occur on high mountain passes, don't hesitate to stick out the old thumb and catch a ride down to safer conditions.

CAMPSITE

With the extra clothing required for cold-weather riding, many cyclists prefer to forego camping for inexpensive rooms. If part of your trip will be in cold climate and part in mild, it's very feasible to mail ahead your sleeping bag and tent. Small post offices will hold packages for you if you keep them informed of your schedule, though often the larger the package, the less enthusiastic response you can expect. Other reliable options include mailing packages to friends, business associates, or even churches. Unless the boxes are totally demolished when they arrive, repack them with your cold-weather gear, and send them back to

your hometown. This method will allow you to experience the best of both worlds.

If you decide to camp during off-season cold weather, it's highly recommended that you do some campsite checking before you go. With reduced budgets being the rule, many national forest and state park campgrounds are cutting the water and closing the gates early in the fall, not to reopen again until Memorial Day. Of those that are open, you should enjoy plenty of peace and quiet (unless it's hunting season).

Give some thought to whether your sleeping bag is really adequate to handle cold weather. You can also wear long underwear, vests, and other extras, but don't expect miracles. Such methods will usually allow you to safely push 10 degrees below your bag rating, though I heartily recommend that you leave at least that many degrees to spare. Your air mattress will certainly not be adequate for sleeping on frozen ground. Plan to go with a good closed-cell foam pad or a top quality self-inflating mattress. Always try to roll out on pine needles or dead leaves, avoiding big slabs of rock like the plague. Cold weather is also where the bivy sack (see "Tents" in Chapter 4) begins to look inviting. The air inside the envelope is warmed by your body heat and can boost the temperature of your sleeping bag by several degrees.

You'll definitely want to throw in a pair of gloves to use around the campsite. While the ones you wear riding can be somewhat bulky, camp gloves must allow you to strike matches, open containers, and the like.

If at all possible, try out your stove in cold weather before you count on it on the road. A stove tends to take on an entirely different personality when freezing weather hits. You'll find that, on the whole, stoves with pumps are superior in the cold to those without. Even if yours seems to do fairly well under such conditions, throwing in a tube of primer paste is not a bad idea. Cyclists using butane should prewarm the stove by sleeping with it. Before firing it up, place it on a small piece of foam padding, and then wrap it in aluminum foil.

The choice of campsites is important in cold-weather touring. Arriving late in the afternoon, try to find a place protected from the wind, yet open to the southeast to catch the morning sun. Since many winter weather systems blow in from the north or west, such a setup should work very well for you. Backing up to the southern or eastern edge of a grove of trees would be ideal.

When breaking camp in the snow, try to spread out your tent and tarp belly up before fixing breakfast, in order to allow some of the moisture to evaporate before packing.

MEDICAL CONCERNS

Hypothermia: This dangerous condition is basically brought about when the body's core temperature drops below 95 degrees. Exposure to a cold rain with the evaporative cooling effect of relative wind can lead the cyclist to hypothermia in temperatures well above freezing. Initial signs may include numbness, shivering, slow reactions, loss of coordination, dilated pupils, drowsiness, and loss of judgment. There may actually even be a feeling of euphoria. Death from hypothermia can occur in a matter of hours.

Should the signs of hypothermia begin to occur, it's imperative that wet clothing be removed as soon as possible. The victim should then be warmed in a sleeping bag or tub of warm (not hot!) water. When using a sleeping bag, it is far more effective if there is another warm body in the bag with the victim; direct body contact provides the maximum amount of correct temperature available under such conditions. Administer hot liquids so long as the person is conscious and get him under the care of a trained medical professional as quickly as possible.

Frostbite: Many people discount the effects of frostbite. Actually, shock, heart failure, and loss of limb due to gangrene may result. If skin becomes a red, flushed color, frostbite may well be on its way. The next stage would bring about a white or grayish-yellow tinge to the affected area. Don't always count on pain being present; some people feel absolutely none. As the severity of the condition increases, the area may feel very numb or cold, with blisters sometimes appearing on a glossy skin surface.

As with hypothermia, the potential for frostbite dramatically increases with humidity and wind. Should you or a riding companion show signs of frostbite, your first move should be to gently cover the affected area. Give warm liquids, and immerse the part in warm water (102 to 105 degrees). The exception to this is if the area has been thawed and refrozen, in which case it should be warmed at room temperature. Despite what you may have heard, do *not* rub the affected area, since this can cause gangrene. If frostbite has occurred to fingers or toes, keep them separated with gauze after rewarming, and exercise the part in "mid air." Don't walk on feet that have just been frostbitten, and don't apply dressings unless the victim is going to be transported. *Do* have a trained medical person attend to the situation as soon as possible.

Besides the precautions mentioned earlier about avoiding cold-related injuries, remember that the likelihood of problems increases after recent illnesses or during periods of fatigue. Booze and cigarettes are no-no's. If you get a room for the night, don't take a shower or bath right before you head out on a cold morning.

11

Taming the Urban Jungle

Most touring cyclists tend to avoid city riding like the plague. It's tough to deal with swerving vehicles, opening car doors, glass, kids, dogs, and pollution after those wonderful stretches of long lonesome highway. But despite some very real threats to health and welfare, the city can be a fascinating diversion for the cycle tourist. The culture, architecture, specialty shops, restaurants, and of course, people, can provide endless parades of sensory diversions. It's hard to get bored riding in the thick of urbania. The key to squeezing enjoyment out of city environments is to have a *strategy* for dealing with each of their unsavory characteristics.

TRAFFIC

The bottom line for surviving in heavy traffic is to go with the flow. Only if you follow the same rules designed for every other vehicle, can you expect the traffic system to work in your favor. Such things as hugging a right-turn lane when you intend to go straight, or making a left turn from the right side of the street because "cyclists have no business in the traffic flow," are foolish and dangerous. (As a matter of fact, such "left from the curb" maneuvers are responsible for three times as many car/cycle collisions each year as turning left from the proper lane.) Following are discussions of several different traffic techniques that should keep you up and riding through the thickest of the urban sprawl.

Where You Fit In

Many cyclists will tell you that the best place for you to be when riding in the city is as far to the right as possible. They are wrong. Flirting with the curb or a line of parked cars can set you up for all kinds of problems, some of which can have very unhappy endings. Let's say, for instance, that you're on a rather narrow two-lane city street, riding over to the right as far as possible. Two cars approach, one from behind, and one from the opposite direction. Since you're perched on the very fringe of the pavement, the driver overtaking you decides he can probably squeak by without causing problems for the oncoming traffic. Halfway past you, he realizes that he has slightly overestimated the width of the roadway. Will he choose to sideswipe the oncoming traffic, or merely crowd you off the road and drive on? Had you been a couple of feet from the edge, the driver would have never had a chance to misjudge the situation. His only option would have been to make a safe, sane pass in the other lane when it was clear.

But that's only the beginning. Suppose that you are passing a line of parked cars, and somebody pulls the old "open the car door" trick on you. If you are less than two car lengths away when it happens, it's highly unlikely that you'll be able to stop in time to avoid hitting the door. To swerve around it is little more than a high-stakes gamble, since there will be no time for looking to see if anything is approaching from behind. Had you been far enough away to just miss the door in the first place, however, you could have kept pedaling smoothly on, rattling neither yourself, nor the oncoming traffic.

If you're still not convinced, consider that a cyclist out from the curb a couple of feet will be seen more easily by traffic pulling out from side streets and will also run less risk of being plowed into by right-turning

RIDING FOR LANE WIDTH

NARROW LANE   **WIDE LANE**

vehicles. And should there happen to be one of those storm sewer grates that can catch a bike wheel (as can happen especially in foreign cities), hugging the curb is the best way to make sure the grate gets you.

Riding out from the curb is *not* meant to be an offensive strategy. You have a responsibility to make sure that you are not severely impeding the traffic flow. If conditions are such that you are holding someone back unduly, by all means pull over and let him pass. On most major thoroughfares, however, you will find that staying a foot or two out from the curb is not going to stall traffic.

Should you happen to be going as fast or faster than the traffic itself (by no means uncommon in many foreign cities), you may want to consider moving out from the curb to occupy an entire lane. In many areas of the world, *any* vehicle (including a bicycle) that is traveling as fast as the traffic flow has a *legal obligation* to operate in the existing traffic channels.

Intersections

By far the most important thing to remember about intersections is to always proceed in the lane that has been designated for the direction you wish to travel. If you are going straight, you should not be in the right-turn lane. If you are turning left, don't attempt it from the right-hand curb. It can all be summed up quite nicely in one sentence: Other than when changing lanes, under no circumstances should your path ever cross the paths of traffic flowing in the same direction. (Your only other alternative for a left turn is to *get off the bike* and walk it straight

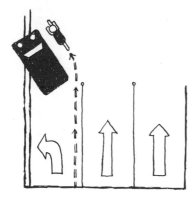

Ride on outside of 'left turn only' lanes

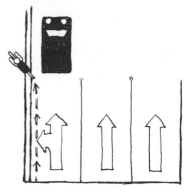

If lane is marked for 'left or straight,' make turn from left or center

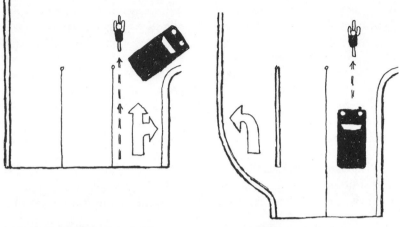

In lane marked for 'straight
or right,' stay inside to
continue straight

If there are no lane
markings, keep to
center of lane

across in the crosswalk, and then cross again *on foot* to the far side. You
are then considered a pedestrian, not a cyclist with an obligation to stay
with the traffic flow.)

If a lane has arrows indicating two different directions, say straight
and right, always be on the side closest to the direction you wish to
travel. For example, you would keep to the right of the lane in order to
turn right, to the left of the lane to go straight. Otherwise, you run the

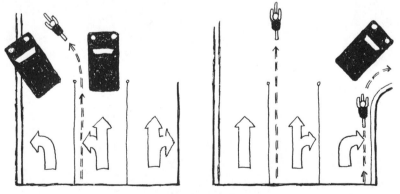

In intersections with more
than one turn lane, ride to
avoid crossing traffic

THE 4 MOST COMMON
CAR/BIKE COLLISIONS

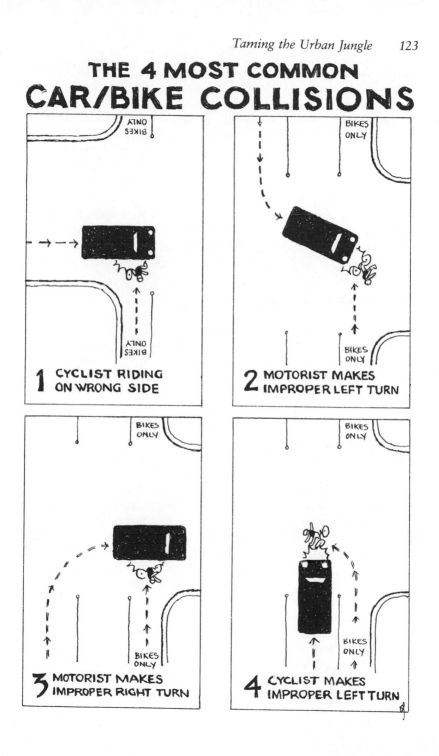

risk of a vehicle making a right-hand turn into your side. This very situation of being channeled toward the right-turn lane will probably be the biggest problem you will encounter when riding in traffic. To avoid such situations, you must look far enough ahead to get an advance feel for the traffic flow, thereby avoiding last-minute lane changes.

By far the safest way to change lanes and proceed from four-way stops is to establish eye contact with vehicle drivers. Merely giving a hand signal and then acting may be legally correct but becomes rather pointless if no one gets the message in time.

Finally, a word about helmets: 75 percent of the cyclists who die in traffic accidents each year (mostly in cities) do so from brain injuries. In urban settings, where there are so many problem-causing intersections, it is hard to imagine a more crucial piece of equipment.

GLASS AND LITTER

Cities and broken glass go together like bread and butter. And since swerving to avoid such debris is extremely dangerous due to traffic, it becomes virtually impossible to miss all of it. Fortunately, however, running through broken glass does not always result in flats—especially if you've mastered the fine art of cleaning your tires with a gloved hand while riding. In theory, it may sound wiser to simply stop after each glass patch and inspect your tires visually. In practice, you'll be lucky to make your way from one end of town to the other before it's time to pack it in and head for home. There is simply too much broken glass for such measures to be practical.

By all means, no one should try to clean a tire with gloves in the city until he has done it countless times on the open road (just as no one should take a drink from a water bottle until he can ride with one hand). In urban areas, restrict your cleaning to the front tire, which is usually what catches most of the debris anyway. Keep your hand completely outstretched, using only the flat portion of your palm against the tire. Of course, this technique is not open to cyclists using fenders.

Many people also use tire savers—those small metal wires that sit at the surface of your front tire and pull debris out of the rubber. The problem with these is that the only way they can work is if the debris is not yet embedded deeply in the tire. Small slivers of glass, staples, and metal points can become firmly embedded on the first revolution of the wheel. While a gloved hand is useless if the debris is completely below the tire surface, the pressure exerted by the hand will drag out many things that tire savers just cannot catch.

Generally speaking, you'll find that residential boulevards have less debris on them than commercial or industrial streets. Be alert at intersections, since there may be windshield, headlight, or taillight glass remaining from a recent accident. (Such glass is often hurriedly swept out of the main traffic lane and left near the curb for bicycles to pick up.) Parking lots remain favorite places for youngsters to thrill to the sound of breaking glass, and lots are usually not swept nearly as often as streets. Though it would seem much easier to avoid debris in lots, trying to figure out their anarchistic traffic flows keeps most of us from paying too much attention to the ground surface.

WHEEL TRAPS

Most cities have replaced the old parallel grate sewer covers that were so dangerous to unwary cyclists. It still pays, however, to keep your eyes totally peeled for such fixtures. Even if you're positive they don't exist in the area where you're traveling, remember that there are many other kinds of grates that can throw you off balance or dent your rims. The most common villains are those that are recessed several inches from the level of the pavement. In heavy traffic, it's not good enough to see them only in time to swerve around them. Bridge expansion joints can be another wheel trap; some will actually require that you get off and walk across.

Tunnels can indeed add a sense of helplessness to the plight of the cyclist. The first 100 yards or so are especially dangerous, since this is where motorists are still getting used to the change in light and driving environment. If there happen to be sidewalks, by all means use them. If not, a leg light, flag, and any reflectors you might have will definitely help your cause. In fact, it's not a bad idea to change into your brightest shirt or jersey before entering a tunnel. Some progressive states have installed motorist warning lights that the cyclist can activate before entering, though these are by no means in widespread use. It is absolutely imperative that you be a competent enough cyclist to ride through a tunnel in an unwavering straight line. Even minor swerves can cause much more psychological havoc with following motorists than the same maneuver would on an open street.

ROUTING

Make no mistake about it—in a large city, routing can make or break you. It is worth as much of your time as it takes to assemble good maps, and then verify your proposed route long *before* you're into the thick of it. I've made the crucial mistake of waiting to determine a route until I was on the outskirts of a large city. There were very few people around to ask, and those I found had no idea of how to get from point A to point B except by interstate! In such cases, the only real way out is to place a call to the city police and ask for help. (How quickly you'll be able to find a phone, though, is another matter.)

The first step in the urban route search is to get your hands on a *good* city map. First try contacting the chamber of commerce, which will probably send you a map of very questionable quality, where all the city attractions are blown up into bizarre cartoons that obliterate the street name information for eight square blocks. If this proves to be the case, contact Rand McNally, which has urban maps for most large cities in the United States (see address in the Appendix). While these maps may not totally solve your routing problems, they are fine for making your way to specific addresses and attractions that probably do not show up on bike path maps. If you need a bike shop, for instance, it often becomes a matter of looking through the yellow pages and matching addresses to your city map.

While the chambers of commerce may not provide freebie city

maps, many will have special bike route maps provided by the city department of transportation. These should be used *in addition* to your city map. If the chamber of commerce is unaware of such offerings, check with the department of transportation itself. Be forewarned, however, that this kind of correspondence can take several weeks, so don't wait until you're ready to take off before you begin the big search.

While we're on the subject of using the chamber of commerce (or in many large cities, the tourist or visitor bureau), you may want to ask if there will be any large celebrations going on the day you plan to pass through. Such occasions, along with big sporting events, can create massive traffic problems. Don't find yourself stuck in the middle.

Organizations are another good source for obtaining city riding information. Bikecentennial's terrific magazine entitled *The Source* offers an incredible selection of route guides, several of which concentrate on specific cities (see Appendix for Bikecentennial address).

As a last-ditch effort, call the city police or local bike shop in the area and ask for routing info. Have your city map in front of you, and be somewhat familiar with at least the main streets before you dial. With a felt-tip high-lighting pen, trace the route as it's told to you over the phone. There are no real guarantees with this method, mostly because you may be talking to someone who has never really ridden such a route himself. It is, however, infinitely preferable to winging it alone.

TIMING

A certain hour of the day or day of the week can mean the difference between a pleasant pedal through a city and a terror-stricken battle with the four-wheelers. If you've never lived in a large city before, it's easy to underestimate the impact of morning and evening rush hours, as well as noon lunch blitzes. *DON'T!* During rush hours, ride only on residential side streets that parallel your route (impossible without a good city map). Should you wind up in heavy traffic, however, be especially cautious about riding into the sun. Many riders will turn on their lights during such times, which can be marginally helpful.

Friday and Sunday evenings can be just as insane. If things get especially bad for you on weekends, it's wise to find out the location of the city's manufacturing center and stick to that. The scenery and road conditions may be less than ideal, but the peace of mind gained is often worth it.

SPENDING THE NIGHT

Cities are places that deserve a little advance research if you plan to spend the night. Have your destination marked on your map, and know just how you plan to get there well before you pass the city limits.

Hostels make very good urban bedrooms, but be sure to check ahead to see if they take nonmembers. Also, ask what time you'll probably need to arrive there to ensure a space. If you plan on using hotels, by all means make a visit to a bookstore for a travel guide that rates the offerings in several price ranges. (This is where those little stars and happy faces really come in handy.) Once you've made a decision, call well in advance for reservations. You never know—there might be a convention of widget salesmen booking the place for the same night. Since you may not be able to get your bike into the room with you, ask the hotel management if they have security closets for their guests.

If, for some strange reason, you find yourself lost in the thick of the concrete jungle with little cash, make a call to a police station and get an appropriate number for one of the city hotlines. These people can then refer you to a local church or mission, Salvation Army post, or some agency that can put you up for the night. By the way, any contribution you can send to such places after you get home will be greatly appreciated.

BAD SIDE OF THE CITY

Every city has its notorious neighborhoods and tough towns that the cyclist should avoid. Of course, few of us ever *plan* our trips to take us through such areas—it's just a natural result of not knowing a thing about the place. This is why you should plan your route carefully, using the people resources previously mentioned. If you get to the edge of a large city and want to make a route check, simply stop at a phone booth and call the local police. They will be able to tell you whether your intended route will take you into any seedy or heavily congested areas and can suggest alternatives right on the spot. They'd much rather deal with you at this point than shuffle a sheaf of papers because you got ripped off on the wrong side of the tracks.

12

Problems of
the Open Road

For most of us, riding the open road is what distance cycling is all about. It's there that cadence, white lines, and countryside all melt together into an almost effortless euphoria—a sense of perfection that makes us pity anyone not similarly attached to the turned-down bar.

Unlike city riding, which can be a white-knuckled affair from start to finish, the problems encountered here often come in brief but intense spurts. Consequently, you may be caught totally off guard, with euphoria being turned abruptly into a cheek-to-cheek dance with the asphalt. If you're a good student and pay close attention, the road will teach you all kinds of worthwhile things: how to judge the size of a vehicle before it catches up with you, and likely areas for dog hangouts, gravel patches, or rough shoulders. But, alas, even the most careful rider will occasionally be unpleasantly surprised. Much like an airline pilot, you will truly earn your keep only when something goes wrong. Keep the following information tucked away on mental file, under "What to Expect When You're Not Expecting Anything."

LARGE VEHICLES

Cyclists and semis aren't usually the best of traveling companions. It takes both courage and stability to hold fast to that shoulder with 20 tons of metal blowing by. And occasionally, it takes a bit of intuition to sense

when you and an 18-wheeler are about to fight each other for the same space. Quite understandably, many cyclists consider logging trucks the ultimate hazard. They are incredibly big, and if the drivers are getting paid by the trip, they will be in an incredible hurry. To top things off, they are usually found screaming along the frightfully narrow, winding roads of the nation's remote woodlands.

For most open-road cycling on hazardous routes, I feel it is actually more dangerous to cling inches from a very rough edge, than to cautiously assert your territory by remaining a foot or two into the lane. The logic here is as basic as it is in the city. If you're barely hanging onto the pavement, many drivers will attempt to brush past you, even in heavy oncoming traffic. Unless the driver is very aware of his vehicle size (unlike many motor-home pilots, who climb into the cockpit about once a year), the results could be tragic. There's been more than one cyclist who was so narrowly missed by a passing vehicle that he lost control and was hit by following traffic. I've actually had my elbow polished by a motor home—a somewhat unnerving experience. Keep in mind, however, that if traffic is simply unable to pass, you should be courteous enough to pull off the road and let people by.

The "territory assertion plan" is practical only when the vehicle behind you can see you well enough to slow down in time to avoid an accident. Being well out into the lane on a blind hairpin turn with oncoming traffic may be asking for it. The potential for catastrophe under such conditions increases proportionately with the size of the vehicle. Be especially alert to two large trucks passing you at the same time. If they see you, adjustments can be made; if they don't, the very least you can expect is to be run off the road.

One valuable tip, straight from a log truck driver's mouth, concerns cycling in large groups. Rather than having people strung out in long single-file lines, ride in groups of two or three, with a good quarter-mile between clusters. This way, trucks can swing around each group and then cut back in quickly, rather than running the risk of having to force a cyclist off the road, should oncoming traffic suddenly appear.

Though it's fairly easy for an experienced cyclist to recognize the sound of a large vehicle from quite far away, many riders prefer to eliminate the guesswork by using one of the various kinds of small mirrors that attach to glasses or helmet. Though these mirrors certainly are limited in scope, I find them most beneficial for noting the position of the car or truck on the roadway. A mirror could conceivably, for instance, warn you of a drunk driver well before he has a chance to annihilate you. There are also mirrors that attach to the handlebars, and others that fasten to the back of your wrist. Many cyclists complain that the former "jumps" whenever the handlebar is turned, and the latter often requires moving your hand at inopportune times. But since no cycling mirror is without disadvantages of one kind or another, either is certainly worth a try.

Truck drivers are usually well aware of the position of their vehicle on the road. If a driver misses you by six inches, it's probably because he meant to. Even under such nerve-racking circumstances, it's your responsibility to hold an unwavering line of travel. As if you couldn't hear them coming, many truckers will give you a blast on their air horns to warn of their approach. This is usually just a courtesy, so don't get upset about it. To those who let out an ear-splitting blow right at your back wheel, however, I sincerely wish 18 flat tires on a Sunday morning in Texas.

Take a firm grip on the handlebars under any truck traffic situation, as the wake of wind will sometimes blow you sideways. The biggest caveat here concerns the problem of over-correcting during a push to the outside. If you are not careful, you could feasibly run into the lane once the truck passes, making you vulnerable to any following vehicle. As for trucks sucking you under their wheels, don't up your life insurance on it. I've never heard of anyone experiencing anything even close to such an effect. If a cyclist goes into the wheels, it would be from over-correcting for a side blow, or a chronic case of the jitters. Both problems can be avoided by keeping a firm, attentive grip on the bike's handlebars during any traffic situation.

A seldom-considered problem with logging and construction trucks concerns the debris they often lose along the sides of roads. Branches, chunks of concrete, rocks, and the like are common hazards along any truck route. Be especially cautious when speeding down the steep, twisted roadways of the Northwest. Sometimes the wind in your ears will muffle the sound of oncoming traffic, so taking a sudden swerve to miss roadside debris can be a real gamble. This is another good case for a mirror.

Check about logging and construction activities every chance you get. If you happen to end up in an especially bad area, remember that weekends are often blissfully void of rumbling trucks. Though I've never holed up until Saturday just to avoid such traffic, I have increased my weekend distances to be out of very bad sections come Monday morning.

POTHOLES

From small ruts and dents to yawning abysses, the world's roads are awash with a million variations on a pothole theme. While potholes certainly can and do cause serious injury to cyclists everywhere, an even more common problem is their tendency to turn round aluminum rims into not-so-round aluminum rims.

As mentioned earlier, when a road has absolutely horrible shoulders, it's probably wiser to ride on the main roadway whenever practical. This is perhaps the biggest reason for planning your trip along lightly traveled backroads. While shoulders may be bad, your chances of riding safely on the right side of the lane is much greater than on primary roads. If you discover that your trip will take you on especially rough roads, perhaps far from good shops, then consider selecting a heavier gauge rim. And, performance fans, be very careful about using high-performance, narrow-gauge spokes when traveling with a loaded bike. They just won't stand up to the rigors of touring. Be especially careful about rim and spoke selection when traveling in parts of Europe with cobblestone roads. You may even occasionally hear tales of European roads consisting of gravel and broken cement slabs. While these roads do in fact exist, it is usually illegal for a bicyclist to ride them anyway. Such wagon roads will be so posted.

An especially dangerous condition exists after heavy rains, since many sizeable potholes will be filled with water. Slight depressions in the pavement will become hidden, often harboring more severe holes and crevices. Travel cautiously through any standing water, no matter how shallow it appears to be.

If you happen to be forced through a particularly rough section of pavement, it may help to stand on your pedals with slightly flexed knees—similar to the way a jockey rides a horse. This posture will allow the shock to be more readily absorbed through the frame, slightly reducing the stress on the rims. Of course, the slower you are going at the time, the better.

CRACKS AND CREVICES

When you stop and think about it, there are an amazing number of dastardly splits hiding in the pavement that can spell disaster for the cyclist.

One villain responsible for a great number of bent rims and bodies is the angled railroad crossing. Under no circumstance should you ever cross railroad tracks at less than a 55- or 60-degree angle. It's just too easy for those unyielding grooves to catch the wheel and either bend a rim or throw you off. Keep a very firm grasp of the handlebars, and slow down to a crawl. Even when crossing tracks at a 90-degree angle, you should be traveling very slowly to avoid pounding your rims into those king-sized troughs that so often exist between the rails and the surface of the pavement.

Bridge expansion joints, discussed for city riding in Chapter 11, can be a problem out in the country, as well. Though most of these joints have been altered so that they will not actually trap a bicycle wheel, some will push and pull the front wheel back and forth a bit. Also, the metal expanders can become very slippery when wet. It's best to treat any bridge as you would a railroad track—very cautiously. Going slowly will also allow you to avoid those sharp pavement drops that are often present on either side of the bridge itself.

Cattle guards are yet another touring trap to be aware of and can be found in virtually any region where grazing animals are a way of life. Be especially alert for cattle guards whenever you see an announcement of "open range." In the western United States, they will often be marked by signs; this is not true, however, in other parts of the world. Sometimes it helps to keep your eyes peeled for the metal bar that *sometimes* runs downward at a 45-degree angle from either side of the guard. If you are competent enough to keep an absolutely steady hand on the bars, you can cross most guards at a crawl without any adverse effects to your wheels. The fact that one wrong slip could sink your bike wheels past the hubs, however, makes many cyclists opt for walking across. This is an especially good idea if it has been raining, since the metal becomes extremely slippery.

Finally, pay particularly close attention when traveling on little-used county roads, especially in regions where temperatures routinely dip below the freezing mark. Large cracks tend to develop in the pavement, and such roads are never high on the priority list for resurfacing. Take your time — both to see the sights and to keep those wheels round.

ANIMALS

If you ask 100 cyclists for the best way to deal with dogs, you'll likely get 100 different answers. After years of wielding pumps, outrunning, negotiating, and barking back at them, I'm convinced that there really is no "best" way. As with people, dealing with man's best friend requires the rider to first size up the animal's personality — and to be prepared for surprises.

I do usually go through certain stages with barking dogs. Stage one is to try to outrun them. Failing at this, I move quickly onto the "primal scream." (A "primal bark" does as well, and either may bring the owner running.) It should be noted that this antic works well only if done early, before the dog gets a chance to stand his ground and take the offensive. A variation of this stage is to also wield a pump, but the resulting loss of control of a loaded bicycle makes this a questionable alternative.

By this time, I've slowed to a crawl and will try all kinds of different commands, in a variety of voice tones. A firm NO! is understood by many dogs and should be used frequently. Often, just the fact that I've slowed down will cause the dog to lose interest in me. If none of this works, I dismount, keeping the bicycle between the animal and me. The key here seems to be to talk and maintain eye contact whenever possible. Once out of the critter's territory, I can usually mount again and ride off.

Repellent sprays are usually effective, but some people feel that they make a dog even more vicious toward the next cyclist. The Animal Protection Institute of America says that while most ammonia-based sprays will not permanently harm a dog, plain water or a water and vinegar mixture in a squirt gun may work about as well. They also suggest staying away from any type of spray that does not list its ingredients on the can.

Kicking at the dog, or turning the front wheel of the bike into it, are definite mistakes, and will often result in your being served for Fido's

lunch — sunny-side up on the asphalt. Though some cyclists carry dog biscuits, I feel I have enough weighing me down when touring without loading up on bribes for dogs. Besides, this seems to encourage dogs to chase cyclists and could lead to a regular county road extortion racket. Then pity the poor person who can't make the payoff!

While dogs are the most common mammalian encounter, other creatures can certainly add their share of spice to the trip. It's not uncommon for a quiet cyclist to surprise a host of wildlife along the edges of the open road. With the larger grazing animals, such as deer and elk, be especially aware of this possibility during early morning and late afternoon hours. If you happen to be riding at night (usually not a wise practice), raccoons, skunks, weasels, and opossums are common and are certainly large enough to cause a fall. Daytime hours may bring snakes and squirrels across your path with absolutely no warning.

Though wildlife-caused accidents are not unheard of, it's far more likely that these woodland residents will come to call at your campsite. Besides bears, which are fairly common throughout much of North America, raccoons and skunks will certainly not hesitate to help themselves while you're busy counting sheep. In addition to the loss of food, your panniers and/or handlebar bag may end up with a few unwanted holes in them if you leave your food on the bike. It's highly recommended that you hang a food pack in a tree.

If you've changed a flat not long before making camp, wipe down the tire with a wet rag, or better yet, with a dab of stove fuel or lubricant. The salty sweat from your hands left on the rubber makes a great "gnawing post" for many small mammals. For the same reason, don't leave your gloves lying around at night either.

Obviously, all garbage should be deposited in an appropriate receptacle. Lacking this, hang it in a tree with your nonbiodegradable refuse, and pack it out with you in the morning.

THORNS

This is a substantial problem in the American Southwest, as well as parts of Spain, Italy, and the Middle East. The typical villain comes from any of several desert plants that each year drop their thorns, which later blow onto the highway. The cyclist traversing much of such terrain would do well to consider using puncture resistant tubes, even though they are somewhat heavy. Suffice it to say that sew-ups are out of the question in such areas and are in fact usually a very poor choice for any serious cross-country trek.

To a certain degree, prevention can be the best medicine when riding in thorny areas. I highly recommend that while riding on a quiet stretch of roadway, you slow down and clean your tires with a gloved hand. You may go through gloves a little faster, but reinforcing the padding stitches when they begin to pull loose should still allow you to get a good deal of service from them.

DETOURS

No doubt about it, detours can be a royal hassle. Besides sending you miles out of your way, they often channel primary road traffic onto dangerously narrow, potholed rural roads. Half the people are upset by the delay, so they tend to try to make up for lost time. Pity you if you happen to get in their way. The only possible solution here is to find out about such conditions ahead of time from the locals, and then avoid these routes during peak traffic times.

When you eat in a restaurant, buy food, or stop for a break, check with the people who live in the area about detours (as well as construction or logging traffic). Many residents will at least know the route conditions within 25 to 50 miles of their homes, so it's not like you have to stop every half-hour for a major consultation. Check for possible alternatives at the mention of bad conditions, since your map may well have skipped the smaller rural roads. If the person you encounter isn't sure of any route but the detoured one, ask someone else! Perhaps it's because service station owners get asked all the time, but they seem particularly knowledgeable about local road conditions. If there's a bike shop nearby, it may be worth the change to call and ask their opinion. Don't forget: some road closures that would preclude automobiles getting through would not necessarily stop a bicycle. Check out this option carefully though, and try your best to make it through before or after work hours.

Remember, all this information can be gleaned in a very few minutes and can save you hours of frustration and dangerous riding conditions. If there don't appear to be any safe alternatives to construction or road resurfacing routes, don't be afraid to stick out a thumb and get past it all with someone else's help. This is not "cheating"; it is a reasonable means of saving your bike and your body from some rather unsavory risks.

GRAVEL AND FALLEN ROCKS

Gravel can be one tough customer. Though it's occasionally possible to steer out of a gravel slide by turning the front wheel in the direction of the skid, doing so successfully with a loaded bike is absolutely the exception rather than the rule. Even if you frequently check on conditions with locals, most non-bicyclists are unlikely to notice loose rock, sand, or gravel on the side of the road. You'll find that the most potentially dangerous areas are downhill stretches with curves. Water runoff during heavy rains can leave substantial amounts of grit on these turns, so the road can go from good to bad at the spin of a crank. The best solution is not only to watch for the debris itself, but for *conditions under which it is likely to occur.*

Steep hillsides in conifer forests or desert areas do not usually hold the soil against erosion as well as deciduous or thick grassland environments. Be especially wary in such areas for the first couple of days after major rainfalls. Another time for caution is when roads have recently been sanded for snowy or icy conditions. In mountainous areas, these conditions can conceivably exist almost any time of year. Again, nearly any local resident can tell you if it has recently snowed on nearby passes.

Other particularly dangerous areas for gravel are near construction sites. Be careful when you see a "Trucks Entering Highway" sign. Loose dirt and gravel can be dragged out onto the main road from the trucks' wheels, and full loads of sand or gravel tend to shed a bit when bouncing onto the highway.

MORE ABOUT MOUNTAINS...

Mountains are also dangerous due to falling rocks, most of which are inevitably hidden around a blind switchback. Look for such debris after *every* rain, and especially as the spring thaw is going on (often well into June). At this time of year it's not a bad idea to keep an eye out for rock actually falling on you. Keep your ears and mirror adjusted, so that any sudden swerves don't bring you into the path of oncoming traffic. There are many mountain roads in the world whose shoulders consist of 12 inches of gravel followed by a 1,000-foot drop. The handling properties of a loaded bicycle make it essential that you cling to the pavement. While normally you would be able to pull over and let an impatient motorist pass, never try it on these shoulderless mountain roads where such a maneuver could be a threat to your safety. If you can see the way clearly for following motorists to pass, wave them around. Truck drivers with any common sense will rarely be a problem on such roads, since they usually have to crawl down mountains, as well as up them.

Wear bright clothing on these roads. Should fallen rock or gravel cause a spill in the traffic lane, it's crucial that you be seen as quickly as possible. Such conditions are not for beginners. Besides the physical fatigue that mountains can induce, they require careful steering and a *controlled descent.* Flying along the downhill side with no thought of the consequences is a quick route to disaster.

Even if you're in good shape, there are definite do's and don'ts for tackling a mountain by bicycle. To begin with, stay in low gears when climbing. If you don't test your gearing ratios on steep grades around your home before heading for the big leagues, you could end up doing a lot of walking, or worse yet, straining a leg muscle. Position yourself

BEWARE OF BLIND CURVES!

toward the rear of the saddle, concentrating power to the downward leg thrusts. On really steep grades, try pulling back on the handlebars with your upper body while pushing forward against the pedals. You may find it helpful to stretch your legs by occasionally standing in the saddle, but be aware that too much sway on a loaded bicycle can cause severe spoke strain.

While climbing in the low handlebar position may seem more comfortable, this actually restricts your breathing. Change hand positions along the top of the bar frequently to avoid arm fatigue, and save the drops for headwind conditions.

Though mountain descents are the exhilarating reward for all your hard work, they also present a great deal of danger. Your trip down *must* be controlled. To avoid overheating of the rims and unnecessary brake pad wear, be sure to pump your brakes at intervals rather than riding them for long periods of time.

The bolts on your rear stays should be checked *daily,* as should the suspension systems on the panniers themselves. And, at the risk of sounding like a broken record, secure your handlebar bags to the front forks with shock cords to avoid loss of steering control on rough descents.

HOSTILITY

Though most riders don't consider it a major problem, there are times when hostile drivers can really throw a wrench into an otherwise beautiful day on the road. Make no mistake about it: some people see the bicycle as no more than a child's toy, something that belongs on the sidewalk or in empty church parking lots. While the number of distance riders and commuters has certainly helped to change this, it is nonetheless an impression that dies hard.

By far the most common trigger for an exchange of unpleasantries is when your presence on the road causes a driver to have to slow down (heaven forbid!). This will most often be on narrow roads where oncoming traffic prohibits a safe pass. Some cyclists actually prefer to be a foot or so out from the edge of the pavement in such cases, just so drivers won't be tempted to pull off a pass that can't be done. While this method certainly has a lot of logic behind it, because of the speeds involved on highways, it should probably be used only when following traffic is light. To hold up an entire string of cars from passing may be legally correct, but you'll merely be fanning the flames of discontent. If you've got a bunch of impatient people behind you, pull over for them. If it happens very often, you should consider rerouting yourself onto less congested roads (see Chapter 6).

I'm not sure if there is a proper response to blaring horns and obscene shouts. If you return the favor, you run the risk of a physical confrontation or a very dangerous game called "run the cyclist off the road." At any rate, you will certainly do nothing to change the person's attitude toward cyclists. The best response in circumstances where the person could easily pass is no response at all. Simply ride in an unwavering line as close to the edge of the pavement as you feel comfortable. Before long, they will get it out of their systems. If you feel that you are in any danger, pull off the road.

Above all, don't let the uncouthness of a few spoil an otherwise good ride. There are plenty of motorists out there who will think that what you're doing is admirable; the impatient road hog is going to squeal loudly at whatever displeases him, be it cyclist, pedestrian, or another motorist. You can help minimize confrontations by always signaling your intentions and keeping your bike moving in a steady line.

There is another type of harassment that you may occasionally run across, especially in rural areas where young residents feel there is a severe lack of entertainment. Rather than be viewed as a bold road adventurer, you could instead be seen as a vulnerable fitness freak in funny shorts. What better entertainment than to poke fun at the new stranger in town? Of course, most of us pay little attention to such pranks, since to do so would be to encourage more of the same. It's far easier, though, to get upset if it happens in a foreign country where we don't understand the language. For some reason we feel that we've been attacked in a more personal manner, and may end up guarding ourselves against people we meet for a long time afterward. With exceptions, there is little difference in the motivation behind being jeered in Istanbul and being jeered in Texas. You are different, and a small group of people prefer to attack what they don't understand.

If someone decides to harass you on the road by creeping behind you and honking or shouting, there are two alternatives. You can stay right where you are (assuming you aren't really holding up traffic) and simply wait for the pranksters to grow tired of the game. The other alternative is to pull over for the louts and end the scenario right then and there. Remember that there will be more chances for such encounters on weekend evenings, when some people seem to enjoy flexing their arrogance.

In short, if you ride in such a manner that allows you to stay a part of the traffic system, but does not unduly prohibit others from doing the same, the harassments you receive will be few and far between. When they occur, realize that because you've chosen a mode of travel that is outside the mainstream, you're going to see many more sides of humanity than you would otherwise. A few of these encounters will be unpleasant; most, however, will be pure and honest pleasure.

13

Bicycle and
Equipment Breakdowns

Even with the best of preventive maintenance, it's almost impossible to escape the occasional breakdown of bicycle or equipment on a long-distance trip. Thankfully, it's rare to encounter a problem that a well-thought-out tool pouch and a bit of repair knowledge can't overcome. The number of cyclists who carry nothing beyond a "third hand" and a set of tire irons and can barely use either, is amazing. Remember: Despite the great popularity that bicycling has gained over the past decade, there are still far more little towns along the road that *don't* have adequate parts and repair knowledge, than do.

Having worked as a mechanic for five years, I'll be the first to admit that many facets of bike repair take a good deal of know-how and skill to perform properly. But the most commonly encountered equipment problems—gears, brakes, flats, and to a certain extent, simple wheel alignments—can be learned relatively easily. If you're afraid to tackle them on your own, there are plenty of shop mechanics who will give you a few Sunday lessons for a reasonable hourly fee. Alternatively, many community centers, parks departments, and cycling clubs sponsor repair classes throughout the spring and summer months. Whichever way you choose to go, it's certain that you'll never regret the hours you invest in learning repairs or the dollars spent for the essential tools to get the job done right.

PARTS

For the beginning tourist, deciding just which spare parts to carry on an extended tour can be more than a little confusing. Of course, some of

what you take will depend to a certain extent on where you will be touring. If you'll be along the Southern California coast, for instance, breaking a part for which you have no spare will probably mean only a short ride or hitchhike to a shop that can replace it. In some parts of the world, on the other hand, such a breakdown could mean traveling hundreds of miles, or waiting for the part to be delivered.

For most of us, our touring routes lie somewhere in between these two extremes. After having the bike thoroughly checked out by a competent mechanic before leaving, take a good long look at which parts are most likely to break, and take replacements for these. Following is a list of those things which you should probably take:

Tire: The additional weight of a loaded touring bike will cause tires to wear out somewhat faster than they would otherwise. This is especially true for the rear, and on longer trips you may want to rotate your tires about halfway through. At first it may sound like a clincher tire would be a difficult thing to pack on a full bike. Not so. Follow the method used in the illustration to fold the tire into a small bundle without damaging the bead. Then merely fasten it onto the outside of your load with a couple of short pieces of rope.

Though more work is involved, using a hand pump to inflate tires is

FOLDING A SPARE TIRE

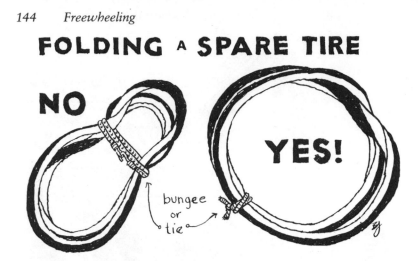

always preferable to relying on the kind of pump found in service stations. These tend to put air in at a very rapid rate, and unless you stop in time, can easily blow the tire right off the rim. If you do have to use a service station pump, keep the air hose on the tire valve for only very brief spurts, and use your own gauge frequently to monitor true pressure.

While we're on the subject of pumping air, I should mention that a good hand pump is a very important piece of your touring ensemble. Under no circumstances should you simply buy the least expensive model, since few of these will be able to even come close to providing the 90 or 100 pounds per square inch of pressure needed in most touring tires. One of the first considerations when purchasing a tire pump is to make sure that it fits the type of valve you have on your tubes. There are basically two different types of valves on today's bicycle tubes: Schrader and Presta.

Schrader is the type of valve used on automobile tires and is by far the most commonly found valve in the United States. The springs in standard Schrader tubes are usually very strong to prevent accidental leakage of air. The problem with this feature is that these valves can be very difficult to pump by hand. Schrader does make weaker-spring valves, but you will have to add them to the tube on your own.

Presta valves are more common in most of the rest of the world. Until recently, they were found only on tubulars (sew-ups) in this country, and the better pumps were designed to fit only this kind of valve. Presta valves use a separate screw nut, which is tightened down after the tires are filled to prevent air loss, and the light springs make pumping by hand

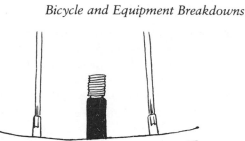

SCHRADER VALVE

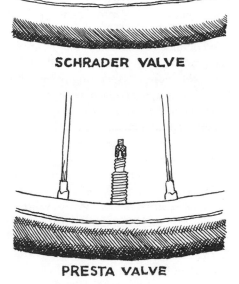

PRESTA VALVE

quite easy. Though most service station pumps will not fit these valves, there are small aluminum adapters available for this purpose.

Whatever pump you choose, make sure that it pumps fairly easily and does not leak air when removed from the valve. These features are still a bit easier to find on Presta pumps, though recent developments in Schrader-style models have begun to offer hope that these two valves will soon be equals. Stay away from pumps that have small hoses that screw into the pump and valve, since these simply offer more places in which leaks can develop. The pump that fastens directly onto the valve may look harder to use, but in the long run you'll find it makes your task far easier.

If you travel in a group and wish to share a pump, make sure that if each rider does not have the same kind of valves, you take an additional pump or special adapter to meet everyone's needs. If you use adapters, try out the pump on each type of valve *before* leaving home. Actually, many touring cyclists prefer not to share pumps and repair kits in groups, since flat tires are a fairly common problem. If everyone has his own supplies, there will be no long delays waiting for the person with the right parts and equipment to show up.

Tube(s): Though you'll be taking a patch kit, there are times when you may develop a leak around the valve itself, which cannot be repaired. Also, if you happen to have a flat in inclement weather, it's easier to throw a new tube in and wait to repair the leak that night in camp. Many cyclists roll their tubes into a tight bundle secured by a rubber band and then store them up under the saddle.

Rear brake and derailleur cables: Though it's rare that a fairly new cable would break, when it does, there is virtually nothing to do but install a spare. One of the more exasperating things about cables is that they have a tendency to fray at the ends, making it virtually impossible to thread them through the housings. You can help prevent this by picking up several plastic cable caps at a bike store and keeping them on all your cables—spares as well as those on the bike itself. In a pinch, a few tight wraps of duct tape will help.

Even if you manage to avoid the fray problem, you'll often have to trim new cables that are too long. There is no way to accomplish this without some sort of wire cutting device. Many cyclists carry a small pair of cable cutters for this reason. If you don't have any, wrap the excess into a tight loop and secure it to your frame where it will be out of your way until you can reach a garage or bike shop. Those cyclists deciding not to carry cutters should probably go ahead and take front *and* rear cables for both brakes and derailleurs. This way, the cable will be a more appropriate length for the specific application, thus keeping the problem of excess wire to a minimum.

Spokes: It's far from uncommon to break a spoke on a long-distance ride. Make very sure that you have the proper sizes for both front and rear wheels. A good way to carry spokes is to wrap them with tape and secure them beneath the chainstays.

Nuts and bolts: It's a good idea to take extra nuts and bolts for racks and pannier suspension systems, derailleur clamps, fingertip shifters, and other parts. Finding extras of some of these parts is not always so easy. (For example, the Allen bolts that attach some racks to the frame can be particularly elusive.) It is extremely important to make a daily check that *all* metal fastening devices are secure. Once you develop a routine for this, it will take very little of your time and could save you a lot of headaches later on. Such a routine is an even more important consideration after traveling on rough roads.

As your touring takes you into more into remote parts of the world, your on-board parts inventory should be increased. You may, for instance, wish to take extra chain links and a rivet extracting tool in case the chain breaks. On rough roads, perhaps two spare tires and an extra spare tube may be worth the weight. Some cyclists even take extra wheel and crank bearings when riding in very remote areas. Of course, there are limits to what you can anticipate going wrong and to the amount of spare parts and tools that you can carry to take care of the problems. You can keep your troubles to a minimum by checking the bike thoroughly before leaving home (repack bearings, align wheels, and the like) and then by keeping a close eye on things every day that you're on the road.

BREAKDOWNS

Following is a discussion of the most common breakdowns you'll experience on the road, how to fix them, and, when feasible, how to prevent them in the first place.

Problem: flat

Equipment: tire irons (two or three), patch kit or spare tube (both should be taken), talc powder, pump (appropriate hub wrenches if bicycle is not equipped with quick-release)

Procedure: First of all, undo the quick release for the appropriate brake. If your bike has no such mechanism, loosen the adjustment barrel enough to allow the tire to slip past the brake shoes after it is reinflated. (Some people prefer to forego such matters and inflate the tire after it has been replaced on the bike. I inflate it before replacing it, because it's much easier to check for proper seating of the tire bead on the rim while the tire is off the bike.) For rear wheel flats, shift down to the small outside rear sprocket. Pull the rear derailleur back while pushing the wheel toward the front of the bike.

Before removing the tire from the rim, try to locate the culprit that caused the problem. Failing at that, remove the tube, keeping it properly oriented to the way it sat in the tire. Run your fingers carefully along the inside of the tire. If you still come up empty, blow up the tube with a little air. Once the leak is discovered, go over that section of the tire again! (Nothing is more frustrating than to get the thing fixed, only to have the same tiny thorn poke another hole in your tube.)

While some cyclists prefer to use a patch kit on the spot, I usually just put in a new tube and patch the hole in camp. This repaired tube then goes in to replace the next damaged one.

If there's any "trick" to repairing flats, it comes when reassembling the tire-tube. Always check to see that the rim strip is in place over the spoke heads. Next, slip one side of the tire onto the rim. Sprinkle the tube with talc powder and insert the valve stem into the rim hole. (This powder will substantially reduce the chance of pinched tubes when you reinflate the tire.) With each hand working outward from the stem in an opposite direction, tuck the tube into the cup of the tire with your fingers. Follow behind with the base of your palm, pushing the tire completely onto the rim. When you've finished, briskly roll the tire and tube back and forth laterally with the palms of your hands until you've circled the entire rim. I promise, IF YOU DO THIS FAITHFULLY, YOU'LL NEVER HAVE A PINCHED TUBE!

As you reinflate the tube, check that the bead of the tire is sitting perfectly just above the rim.

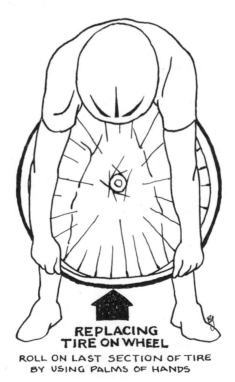

**REPLACING
TIRE ON WHEEL**
ROLL ON LAST SECTION OF TIRE
BY USING PALMS OF HANDS

Prevention: Glove your tires whenever you run through glass or similar debris. Check at camp for bits of rock or glass embedded in the tire. Replace tires when tread is worn.

Problem: broken spokes

Equipment: tire irons, spoke wrench, talc powder, hub wrenches if wheels are not quick release, spokes, and nipples. (For right side of rear wheel, you'll also need a cog remover and wrench to fit it.)

Procedure: The first steps of this operation are identical to those taken to repair a flat. The problem encountered most often occurs when trying to replace a spoke on the cog side of the rear wheel. Sprocket clusters tighten on the wheel as you ride, often requiring Herculean effort to remove. The giant wrenches that work so well to give you leverage are obviously not practical to carry on the road, so you may find yourself hitchhiking to the nearest gas station with the wheel, in search of a mammoth adjustable. When replacing the cog, always grease the hub threads to make removal as easy as possible the next time around.

Make sure that you have the proper length and gauge spokes for both the front and rear wheels. They are not necessarily interchangeable! After replacing the broken spoke, tighten only enough to give it tension, finishing the job when the wheel is back on the bike. Make sure that no part of the spoke protrudes past the lip of the nipple. Reassemble the wheel as per the steps for changing a flat.

If I could choose one tool to spend a little extra money on for quality, it would be my spoke wrenches. (The best ones fit only one gauge, so you may need a couple.) If you get a stubborn nipple, it takes very little twisting from a cheap wrench to strip it, causing endless headaches when trying to align a wobbly rim. You should check the alignment of your wheels every morning before riding, so it won't take long to get your money's worth.

Prevention: Don't use a racing gauge spoke for touring. You may get by fine on the front wheel, but the added weight on the rear can cause some real problems. If at all possible, avoid hitting potholes and railroad tracks at anything but a crawl. Keep your wheels properly aligned. And finally, be careful if you like to climb hills standing up. Too much lateral sway will pop a tight spoke.

Problem: aligning the wheel

Equipment: quality spoke wrenches (see above)

Procedure: If there is one item of maintenance that strikes fear in the heart of the cycle-tourist, it's aligning wheels. Unless the wheel is in very

ALIGNING THE WHEEL
Use brake pads as alignment guide

TO MOVE RIM TO THE
LEFT:
Loosen appropriate
spokes on **RIGHT**side
and tighten matching
spokes on **LEFT** side
the same amount.

TO MOVE RIM TO THE
RIGHT:
Loosen appropriate
spokes on **LEFT** side
and tighten matching
spokes on **RIGHT**side
the same amount.

IMPORTANT:
Do not adjust more than
½ turn at a time!

bad shape, however, you'll find that a patient, cautious approach will usually yield favorable results. Operate in small increments, preferably no more than a quarter turn per spoke to start.

It helps to take a minute to think of just what you're doing to your wheel every time you turn a spoke. Most obvious is that tightening a spoke on one side of the rim tends to pull it over in that direction. But that also means that you're increasing the tension on the spoke directly opposite. If you do nothing but tighten, you'll end up with a "flat" spot. Remember, the rim can be moved toward the hub, as well as from right to left. To solve a small wobble, then, tighten the spokes *slightly* on the cupped side, while loosening those on the opposite bulge an equal amount. After making sure your brake pads are centered around the rim, use them as your guide for truing the wobbles. Check the effects of each quarter-turn. (Keeping the spoke between the brake pads, turn the nipple wrench clockwise to tighten it, counterclockwise to loosen.)

If you find that the side to be loosened is already loose, tighten these spokes a half-turn or so before beginning. If, however, the side to be pulled over is already very tight, you've probably got a bent rim. For this you must either pull the rim over, starting well away from the bulge (a sometimes complicated affair), or wobble to a shop.

Prevention: same as for broken spokes

Problem: gear adjustment, broken gear cable

Equipment: small screwdriver to fit high and low adjusting screws on front and rear derailleurs, wrench to fit cable anchor bolts (usually 8 or 9mm), pliers

Procedure: Believe it or not, derailleurs are amazingly simple mechanisms. And unless you happen to take a nasty spill and re-sculpt yours, it should take you no more than a few minutes to become a veritable expert.

About the only two adjustment scenarios you should run across are: the chain will not go into (a) high gear (small sprocket on rear, large on front, or (b) low gear (large sprocket on rear, small on front). Take a minute to watch the inside action of your derailleurs as you move your shift levers. If you either pull the cable as tight as it can get, or give it all the slack it has, you'll notice that the movement of the mechanism is limited by two small set screws. Following these to the exterior, you'll probably see that one has an "L" beside it (for low), and the other an "H" (for high). When you turn either low screw in, you are simply reducing the amount of "play" available to the inner mechanism. Turning either one out, or loosening, extends the range.

If your chain won't climb up on the large rear sprocket, for example, it's usually because the low-gear adjusting screw is turned too far in, prematurely limiting the mechanism's movement. Both front and rear derailleurs work essentially the same. Be especially careful that, in order to solve the problem of not getting into the large rear sprocket, you don't extend the range of the derailleur so much that it carries the chain into the spokes. If you can't get into this gear after loosening the adjusting screw, your derailleur is either bent or is too small to handle the size of your gear cluster.

There should be no real slack in the cables when your shift levers are moved all the way forward. If there is, simply loosen the appropriate cable anchor bolt, pull the cable snug with a pair of pliers, and retighten. This is essentially the same procedure necessary for cable replacement, though you should first wipe a thin film of grease along the cable before installing. Sometimes during this installation procedure it's possible to unknowingly pull the wire so tight that you end up shorting the derailleur from the cable it needs. Thus the bike will not shift into the small rear sprocket, and no amount of loosening of the high-gear adjusting screw will work.

Remember that a new cable will stretch. After installing one, firmly move the shift lever back and forth while the bike is stationary to work out the stretch. Loosen the anchor bolt, pull until snug, and retighten.

GENERIC DERAILLEURS

(FRONT AND REAR NOT TO SCALE)

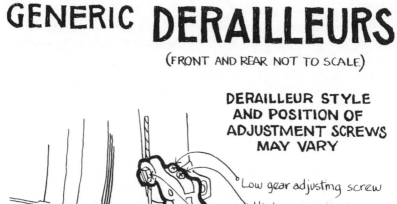

DERAILLEUR STYLE AND POSITION OF ADJUSTMENT SCREWS MAY VARY

Low gear adjusting screw

High gear adjusting screw

Cable clamp bolt

FRONT

REAR

(High/low gear adjusting screws may be here)

Cable-adjusting barrel

Low gear adjusting screw

High gear adjusting screw

Prevention: Keeping your derailleurs free from dirt and lubricated with a fine chain oil will go a long way in eliminating shifting problems. Wiping a thin film of grease on all cables before installing them will prevent rust, especially where the wire is surrounded by a housing. Keep a cap on your cables to avoid fraying.

Problem: brakes out of adjustment, broken brake cable

Equipment: "third hand," pliers, appropriate wrenches for brake pad assembly, and cable anchor bolt

Procedure: Most brakes, whether side-pull or center-pull, can be a pain to adjust until you've done it a few times. Patience and a "third hand" are necessities.

When the brake cables have slipped to the point where they can no longer be rescued with the adjusting barrel, it's time to get out the tools and go to work. The first thing you should always do before proceeding is to make sure that the adjustment barrel is several turns from being all the way in.

Begin by adjusting the brake pads so that they rest properly against the rim. The bottom of the pad should be perfectly parallel to the rim, meeting the metal just barely above the spot where it curves under to form the horizontal surface.

Next, attach the "third hand" to the brake and loosen the cable anchor bolt. If it is a center-pull, place the pair of pliers under the anchor assembly, leaving just enough room for your thumb of the same hand to rest between the pliers and the bottom of the assembly. As you pull the cable down with the pliers until it is snug, use your thumb as a lever to push up against the anchor assembly. Now with the proper wrench in your other hand, tighten the nut enough to hold the cable in place. Releasing your pliers, put another wrench on the opposite side of the anchor nut and tighten. The assembly should be quite snug, though it is possible to snap the aluminum bolt if you get carried away. This technique is very effective at getting the maximum amount of cable tautness. For this reason, don't pull downward too hard on the cable with the pliers or your brakes will end up plastered to the rim after you remove the "third hand." This is why I said earlier to leave the adjustment barrel out a few turns.

Side-pulls are easier to adjust, since the cable anchor assembly is solidly attached to the brake arm. No "thumbing" is necessary to maintain proper tension.

A new cable will stretch, so expect to repeat the above procedures after squeezing the brakes hard several times.

If the brake is not centered around the rim, first check to see that the brake assembly is not hanging off to one side. If it is, loosen the nut assembly on the rear and reposition the brake. If the assembly is centered, then the problem lies with the wheel not being true or the fork being bent. You can artificially center the assembly from the rear or loosen the brake cable adjusting barrel to compensate. On a side-pull, it is possible to hold a thick screwdriver blade against the brake spring on the side of the bulge and strike it firmly with a hammer. This should be a last resort, however, since it weakens the spring. In reality, you're simply off-centering the brake to match the off-centered wheel. Better to head for a bike shop.

Prevention: Periodically tighten the brake cable anchor bolts. Since most are aluminum or cheap steel, however, use care not to snap them in two. Keep the cables covered with a thin film of grease to prevent rust. Pump your brakes on long descents to avoid damaging the brake pads.

Problem: hub cones out of adjustment

Equipment: set of appropriate cone wrenches (as well as axle nut wrenches, if wheel is not quick-release)

Procedure: It's very important to make periodic checks of how the axle is riding in the hub. An axle that is too loose or too tight could actually damage the hub — in many bikes, an expensive piece of equipment to replace.

The initial check for loose cones is as easy as picking the bike up off the ground and trying to move the wheel back and forth. At most, there should be only the very slightest bit of side-to-side play (better hubs will seem to have none). Alternatively, you can check for the cones being too tight by bringing the valve stem up almost to the top of the wheel, then seeing if its weight is enough to start the wheel turning. Ideally, the valve stem should spin the wheel back and forth like a pendulum, with no drag or jerky movements.

How you go about adjusting the cones depends upon whether you have quick-release hubs or axle nuts. The wrenches are used on only one side of the axle, and the other side must somehow be kept from turning while the work is being done. With axle nuts, you can simply keep one side snug against the forks while you work on the other. Quick-release owners, however, do not have this option. If you're riding alone, you may want to take a small pair of Vise Grips along. Remove the wheel, clamp the grips to the lock nut on one side, then hold the grips between your legs while performing the adjustment. There will, of course, be no need for such maneuvering when riding with another person, since he can

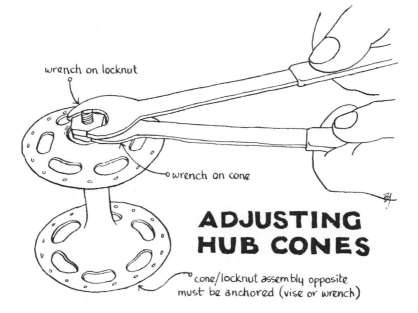

wrench on locknut

wrench on cone

ADJUSTING HUB CONES

cone/locknut assembly opposite
must be anchored (vise or wrench)

simply hold an adjustable wrench against the axle nuts on the other side.

The actual adjustment is relatively easy. Secure one of the thin wrenches to the cone, and one to the lock nut. If the hub has too much play, loosen the lock nut while firmly holding the cone. Then simply screw the cone in a half-turn and snug the lock nut up to it again. The opposite procedure is followed if the cone is too tight. It will probably take you several tries to get it just right, but stay with it until you do. It should be a long time before you'll have to do it again.

Prevention: After you adjust your cones, make sure that the lock nut is well tightened. This will ensure that the operation does not become a daily affair.

Problem: cotterless crank too loose or too tight

Equipment: special lock ring spanner wrench, thin open-end wrench or special spanner to fit bearing cup

Procedure: To check for excess play in the crank, simply remove the chain from the front sprocket and grab hold of one of the crank arms. There should be only the very slightest side-to-side movement in the assembly. At the same time, the crank should spin freely without "snagging." To adjust for side-to-side play, take your spanner wrench and loosen the lock ring from the left side of the bike. Now simply rotate the bearing cup clockwise a half-turn with the appropriate wrench, and snug up the lock ring once again. For a crank that is too tight, the procedure is exactly opposite.

Prevention: As with cone adjustments, the lock ring must be tightened securely if the adjustment is to last. There may be no way to prevent such bearing guides from needing periodic attention, but servicing them promptly will at least keep you from experiencing outrageously expensive problems later on.

14

Making the Best
of Public Transportation

Arranging for the commercial transportation of your bicycle can serve as a wonderful acid test for those considering a career in a travel agency. How else could you get such a feel for airline agent double-talk, bus transportation referrals and re-referrals, and information that has all the consistency of a presidential candidate's speech portfolio?

Yes, your 10-speed partner can cause you more than a little trouble on this one. And since there seem to be no two commercial transportation carriers that handle bikes the same way, don't expect past experience to count for much. While I unfortunately can offer you no absolutes here, I can at least give you a list of the variables you're likely to encounter. Such information will become valuable when it comes time to pick up the phone and enter the transport twilight zone.

AIRLINES

Well, let's jump right into the thick of things. Nowhere will the requirements and means of handling your bike be more inconsistent than on commercial airlines. While writing this chapter, it was tempting to include a company-by-company list of guidelines for you to refer to when preparing to fly with your bike. I half-dismissed the idea because it seemed that it would become dated too quickly. I fully dismissed it when, in trying to verify information given to me earlier, I started receiving entirely different sets of rules from the same airlines. Let's take a look at the "averages" in the various categories that will be of concern.

Charges

The costs of flying your bike from point A to point B will vary from a $5 charge for excess baggage, to a flat fee of $20. With some carriers, this includes the packing box. You should, however, be sure to call the airport ahead of time and ask them to set a box aside, since "we just ran out" is not an uncommon line. If the service fee does not include packaging material, expect to pay $5 to $15 for it. Remember that most airlines will count your bike as one piece of your allotted luggage. Make sure that this is the case and that the thing isn't going as air freight! Remember too that changing airlines will often add extra charges to the trip.

Packaging

A few air carriers use plastic bags for bike transport, and a couple of the smaller ones don't require anything but that the pedals be removed and the handlebars lowered. The vast majority, however, demand the bike be boxed. If you get your own box, *be sure* to first call the airline for the maximum size allowances. To miss by even a couple of inches can lead to grief. The following packaging procedures should get your bike through all but the worst of the infamous bungling baggage handlers.

First of all, deflate the tires to prevent their exploding in a non-pressurized cargo section. Remove the pedals and seat, and shift the rear derailleur into the largest sprocket to minimize the possibility of its getting bent.

Take off the front wheel (along with any fenders or racks) and disconnect the front brake cable at the anchor bolt. Remove the stem and handlebars by unscrewing the stem bolt a good half-inch and striking it downward sharply with a hard object.

Secure the front wheel to the left-side center of the frame's "diamond," being sure to pad the areas where the rim might rub against the rear frame stays. The crank arm can be carefully woven between the spokes, and the wheel tied at various points with twine. The handlebars can then be hung across the top frame tube, with one of the drops protruding through the spokes of the front wheel. (This is why the front brake cable was removed from the anchor bolt. If you have unusually long cables or a very small frame, this step may not be necessary. Remember, though—pulling too tightly on this cable causes stress at the point where it attaches to the brake lever. Do this too often, and you may one day find yourself without a front brake.)

Make a protective padding out of cardboard and tape, and cover the rear derailleur, front fork ends, and wheel axles to prevent them from rubbing through the box. Use plenty of rags to wrap around any likely abrasion spots, as might occur between the handlebars and the top frame tube. A small block of wood stuck between the front forks will help brace them against any sharp blows. These, as well as plastic versions of the same thing, can be found at most bike shops. Package the seat, pedals, and other leftovers in a plastic bag and slip them between the front fork and bottom bracket. Fill in remaining spaces with items like panniers and bicycling shoes. Be sure to close the box securely with strapping tape, marking "this side up" in big letters on both sides.

The above method will allow you to compact your bike so that it meets the *minimum* box size requirements on a public carrier. Some carriers, of course, do not have such stringent regulations. By checking (and rechecking) first, you may be able to meet the carrier's requirements without all of the above work. Generally, though, you should always be prepared to at least remove the pedals, turn the handlebars and stem, and drop the saddle and seat post.

Before you dive into disassembling or assembling your bike at a busy public terminal, ask a nearby airport or airline employee where the best place is for you to begin your task. If you should happen to pick a spot that suddenly begins to get a lot of passenger traffic in the middle of your mess, you could be asked to move, which is much more difficult after the operation has begun. Wherever you work, try to keep all the parts and tools very close at hand, both for the safety of others and to minimize the possibility of lost or stolen items.

When you think that you have the bike reassembled again, don't throw that box away until you have gone through it *thoroughly*. It's easy to have a glove or spare part find its way into the folds of the packing material and get thrown away. A two-minute check can save you time, money, and miles later on. (If you happen to be cycling on foreign soil, you'd do well to check with the airline before leaving the airport to see if boxes will be available for your flight back. Unfortunately, most airports have no facilities to store your original box, so that option is out. If the airline does have boxes at their foreign base, they'll likely tell you to call a day before your scheduled return trip to have one set aside. If they don't have them, check with another major airline.)

While flying is often the easiest kind of connection to make with your bike, problems can begin when you get ready to ride out of the airport. At busy terminals, traffic can be so heavy that it becomes confusing at best, dangerous at worst, to wind your way toward the open road. When you arrive, it's a good idea to try to find a map of the airport that indicates the names of the various in-bound and out-bound traffic arteries. Next, check with either the airport manager's office or an airline or car rental agent for explicit directions about getting to your destination *from the front of the terminal building*. (If there are no maps to put with the directions, have the person draw you one.) When departing, you may want to first walk your bike on the sidewalk to the end of the terminal's airline signs and then begin riding. This way you can avoid the crazy starts, stops, and swerves that are so common at passenger terminal drop-off points.

Be especially cautious about early morning and late afternoon rides out of the airport, since this is often a very busy time for business flights. People who fly on business often time their arrival at the airport very closely. Because of this, the terminal can have all the appearances of a full-blown rush hour.

Liability

Before you take to the friendly skies, be sure to ask if the carrier assumes liability for damages incurred en route. Many do not and some even require you to sign a form stating such. If this is the case, make a call to your insurance agent to see if you're covered. As often as not, you won't be unless you've taken out a special policy commonly referred to as a "rider" (nothing to do with "riding" a bike.) Not to invite trouble, but it isn't a bad idea to have a witnessed "statement of condition" form filled out on or near your date of departure.

BUS

Though motor coaches have a slight reputation for losing things, most people report satisfactory service in sending their bicycles via the racing dog. The packaging requirements are to use a standard factory bicycle box and prepare the bike in the manner described above. Prices for bus transport vary with weight and distance shipped, and, to a certain extent, what state your package is in at the beginning and end of the trip. A run across the country would typically cost between $50 and $75. If your bike is making a trip without you, buses are the cheapest public carrier available.

TRAIN

Amtrak is one of the few public carriers that makes it easy to travel with a bike. Simply package it in a standard bike box (they will provide one the size of a small garage for $5), and your ride rides free. It counts as one of three pieces of luggage, and with a 150-pound weight limit, even the most robust clunker would have little trouble getting aboard. It's a sane, simple way to go—with few surprises. The one important thing to remember about Amtrak, however, is that it will *not* insure a bike against damage if other things are packed in the box with it.

Before selecting Amtrak, you should contact the station from which you're planning to depart to make sure they handle baggage, and also that they will be opening the baggage car at the stop where you intend to get off. At the same time, you can ask if they have any used boxes lying around. If they do, you can expect to get it free of charge.

DRIVE-AWAYS

Though sometimes limited for a cyclist's purposes, automobile transportation companies are so great that I feel obliged to mention them. Most often, they are a service for people who have recently moved and do not wish to pay a motor carrier an outrageous fee for the transportation of their vehicle. By matching up cars to willing drivers, their client gets the car, and you get at least close to where you want to go. These companies can be found in the yellow pages under "Automobiles—Transporters" or "Automobiles—Drive-Away Companies."

Begin by calling each firm to see which one has a vehicle going toward your destination that fits your time slot. It's a good idea to contact them two weeks before you need the car, so that even if nothing is scheduled for that date, they can hold a vehicle for you if one becomes available. The first time you drive, you'll have to fill out a detailed form, be fingerprinted, and provide two references (local if at all possible). Twenty-one is usually the minimum age. If you're traveling with a companion (one is usually the limit), he will have to go through the application procedure as well.

Before hitting the road you'll be asked to surrender a $100 deposit, which is then returned to you upon delivery of the car. The tank is full when you leave, and that's how you're expected to deliver it. (If the vehicle happens to be a guzzler, the company should provide a gas allowance to compensate for the extra cost.) Though they expect you to travel from A to B in a relatively straight line, there will usually be a 15 percent spread for additional mileage.

The biggest catch to all this often concerns your bicycle; many companies won't allow you to take one. If the person on the other end wants his or her car badly enough, though, they will usually agree to your bringing it along. Just remember that the repair of any scratches, dents, or grease marks will come out of your pocket. But even if the bike can't go, sending it via bus and taking a drive-away yourself is usually cheaper than both of you opting for air passage aboard the silver bird.

15

Avoiding the One-Burner Blues

If you're eating a well-balanced diet at home, there should be no reason to alter it dramatically when you hit the road. On the other hand, if your eating habits are *not* what they should be, climbing on the saddle and pumping pedals for 60 miles will let you know about it in a hurry. Admittedly, there is a veritable jungle of claims made for and against things such as carbohydrate loading and high-protein drinks. But unless you're racing (and often even then), there's rarely a need to look too far beyond what can be furnished with wholesome meals from the local market. Let's sum up a few of the touring cyclist's needs and the best means of satisfying them:

Carbohydrates: While a totally inactive person could probably do quite nicely with few carbohydrates, not so the long-distance cyclist. For you, carbos are the best source of energy available. They are much more easily digested than other foods and can help provide a more regulated water supply to the body. As a bonus, carbohydrates tend to be inexpensive.

There are two kinds of carbohydrates: simple (such as table sugar) and complex (such as cereals, beans, and bread). Each is eventually broken down into glucose, the basic form of stored energy. So why not just eat foods loaded with sugar, as opposed to the latter grouping? For one thing, complex carbos are also rich in other body essentials, such as fiber, vitamins, and minerals. Sugars may provide energy, but they are typically referred to as "empty calories," since they offer little else.

Eating refined sugar for "quick energy" can definitely give you a lift. If you overdo it, however, your pancreas may react by secreting excess insulin. This insulin, combined with the extra physical demands of bicycling, can cause your blood sugar to drop to a low level—a condition known as hypoglycemia. (But this condition rarely occurs in healthy people.) You can conceivably end up feeling more sluggish *after* eating simple sugars than you did beforehand. For optimum performance, try to obtain at least half of your calories in the form of complex carbohydrates.

Protein: If you are like most Americans, you're already getting two to three times the amount of protein your body needs. An average 150-pound person generally needs no more than 60 grams of protein per day. This could be obtained from 10 ounces of meat, as well as through daily combinations of vegetables, cheeses, nuts, and grains. Eating a wide variety of foods will best ensure that your nutritional needs are met and give you the necessary amino acid balance. The advantage of not relying on meat entirely is that it reduces your intake of cholesterol and other fats that generally require more time and effort to digest.

Vitamins: Generally, you should try to arrange your diet according to what is known as a "2-2-4-4" schedule: two servings of dairy products, two protein servings, four fruit or vegetable portions, and four cereal and grain portions. (These servings are really quite modest. A small apple, for instance, would count as one of your fruit group.) By following such a schedule, there really is no need to be overly concerned about popping additional vitamin pills. If you use any supplement, one good daily multiple with iron should suffice.

EATING STRATEGIES

Though the morning meal is perhaps your most important one when cycle-touring, it may not be the best idea for you to wolf down a three-pound "lumberjack breakfast" and expect to start climbing mountains. Generally, carbo meals like pancakes will digest more easily on the road than large quantities of high-protein foods such as meat. Then again, you may feel that a little protein may "stick to your ribs" better. The egg batter in French toast lets you have the best of both.

As is true in hiking, it's usually preferable to eat small quantities several times a day than to attempt to consume a big meal at lunch time. This will ensure that your system gets a constant supply of glycogen and will eliminate that sluggish afternoon feeling spawned by those infamous "all you can eat" lunch buffets.

As for cold-weather riding, there should be no need to increase your daily caloric intake by more than five percent, if you are adequately clothed.

RECIPES

Breakfast

The following recipes are designed for two people. For more or fewer persons, adjust the quantities of ingredients accordingly.

SONORA SUNRISE

4 large eggs
2-3 ounces cheese
picante sauce
4 flour tortilla shells
   optional:
sour cream
avocado

Scramble the eggs with two ounces of water. As they begin to firm, add cheese. When fully cooked, place eggs in tortilla shell, add picante (and sour cream, avocado, if desired). Roll up shell, spoon more picante sauce over top. Serve with fruit or juice.

PANCAKES

1 box Bisquick
2 medium bananas
1 cup granola

Merely follow directions on the box of Bisquick. Many fast-food chains that serve breakfast will have small containers of syrup. Ask for a couple of extras the next time you eat at one. Other good topping alternatives are peanut butter, jelly, honey, canned or fresh fruit, and yogurt.

Or for even better cakes:
Prepare at home for each batch of 14 pancakes:

1 1/4 cup all-purpose flour
1 tablespoon baking powder
1 tablespoon sugar
1/2 teaspoon salt

At camp:
Combine one egg, one cup milk, and two tablespoons shortening or oil with premixed dry ingredients and mix until moist, but lumpy. Fry until golden brown on each side, flipping only once.

CANTALOUPE ISLAND

1 medium cantaloupe
1 cup plain yogurt
granola
4 tablespoons honey

If there's a stream nearby, place the cantaloupe in to chill the night before. (If you plan to be near streams often, take a couple of hosiery stockings with you. They're great for stream-chilling berries, containers of yogurt, and the like.) Slice the cantaloupe down the middle and remove seeds. Add to each half the yogurt, granola, and honey. Adding other fruit, such as strawberries or blueberries, will make it even better.

OMELETS

4-5 eggs (for 2 servings)
1/3 cup water
salt
pepper

If you have a no-stick skillet, you won't need any margarine or oil. If not, plan on carrying a small plastic container with vegetable oil. After mixing water, eggs, and seasonings, pour the mixture into the pan and tilt to distribute it an inch up the sides. As it cooks, occasionally lift one of the sides and let the uncooked egg flow to the bottom. When the top of the omelet has firmed up, add any of the following combinations:

Cheddar cheese, tomatoes and sprouts
mushrooms, onions, and Parmesan (Parmesan is easy to carry)
cottage cheese, tomatoes, and sprouts
Monterey jack and diced jalapeño peppers

OATMEAL PLUS

4 packages instant oatmeal (regular is cheapest)
2 peaches or nectarines
4 tablespoons honey

Add fruit and honey to dry oatmeal. Add boiling water and stir. This goes well with an open-face peanut butter sandwich.

ROLL-UPS

4 flour tortilla shells
peanut butter
honey
cinnamon and sugar

Spread peanut butter across the face of a flour shell. Place in skillet on medium heat for one minute. Add honey, cinnamon, and sugar. Slide from skillet onto plate and roll up. Great with juices of all kinds.

CHEESE FRAZZLES

1/2 pound Cheddar cheese
cinnamon bread
applesauce

Cut cheese into slices and place in a *no-stick* pan on medium heat. As oil from cheese begins separating, flip and cook other side. Place on cinnamon bread and top with applesauce.

Lunch

Since lunch is more often than not a "no-cook" meal, here are some suggestions for quick, nutritious fare:
cheese, fruit, and bread
cream cheese on bagels with tomatoes, avocados, and sprouts
cream cheese on bread with celery and raisins
yogurt with fruit and trail-mix granola
cheese, hard rolls, and celery stuffed with peanut butter
banana sliced lengthwise and each half loaded with peanut butter
    (and honey if desired), wrapped in flour tortilla shell
For guacamole sandwich spread, mix:

2 ripe avocados
juice of 1 lemon
garlic salt
chili powder and black pepper to taste

If you don't mind boiling a little water, add a cup of instant soup or Top Ramen to any of the above.

Dinner

LENTIL SOUP

Combine the following ingredients in plastic bags at home, and mail ahead to post offices along your route:

1 cup dried lentils
1 teaspoon celery salt
1 bay leaf
2 tablespoons dried minced onion
4 bouillon cubes

At camp, boil 4 cups of water, and add:

1 package freeze-dried carrots
1 cup canned tomatoes
1 tablespoon oil
above premixed ingredients

Cover and cook on low heat for at least 30 minutes. Serve with bread and cheese.

QUICK MAC DINNER

Prepare according to directions 1 box of macaroni and cheese. After draining water, add:

1 small can tuna
1 small onion
1 small can peas

Top with croutons and serve with salad or fruit.

THE BASIC BURRITO

After warming one can of refried beans, spread one-half cup on the center of a flour shell, and garnish with avocado, Cheddar cheese, sour cream and picante sauce.

Roll up and serve with corn on the cob (fixed earlier and wrapped in foil) and salad.

SPUD HEAVEN

Fry two medium-sized potatoes until brown, with with one egg, one fresh tomato, a small bell pepper, onion, and mushrooms. Five minutes before serving, top with crumbled Cheddar cheese. Serve with salad and fruit.

RAMEN SUPREME

2 packages chicken-flavored Ramen noodles
2 cans boneless, precooked chicken
1 small onion
1 small bell pepper
1/4 pound fresh mushrooms

After cooking noodles according to directions, add the package of seasoning included with the noodles, along with the above remaining ingredients. Cook for five minutes on very low heat, stirring occasionally. Add a little soy sauce and dig in.

And over rice . . . You may well find quick-cook rice to be one of your best friends on the road. Cook up a couple of cups and set aside. Then: saute onions, zucchini, tomatoes, green pepper, and mushrooms (and bits of shredded beef jerky, if you like). Pour over rice and top with grated Parmesan cheese. For an even easier dish, heat up a can of chunky soup and pour it over your quick-cook rice.

Sauces

WHITE SAUCE

Can be used to add a gourmet touch to almost any dinner entree.

1 cup milk
2 tablespoons flour
2 tablespoons butter
1/4 tablespoon salt
1/8 tablespoon pepper

Melt butter and add flour and salt. Then pour in milk, stirring rapidly until smooth.

SWEET AND SOUR SAUCE

Heat:

1/3 cup pineapple juice
3 tablespoons vegetable oil
2 tablespoons brown sugar
1 teaspoon salt (or soy sauce)
1/2 teaspoon pepper
1/4 cup mild vinegar

Desserts

GRAHAM CRACKER SURPRISE

Spread graham cracker with one tablespoon of cream cheese and a similar amount of strawberry preserves.

MOCK APPLE PIE

2 medium tart apples, pared and sliced
2 tablespoons water
1/2 teaspoon lemon juice
1/2 teaspoon cinnamon
1/4 cup brown sugar
3 tablespoons flour
2 tablespoons butter or margarine
1/4 cup granola

Place apples in ungreased skillet. Sprinkle on water, lemon juice, and cinnamon. Mix remaining ingredients until crumbly and add to apples. Simmer on low heat until apples are tender. If desired, top with plain yogurt.

NO-BAKE COOKIES

Mix together and boil:

> 2 *cups sugar*
> 1/2 *cup milk*
> 1/2 *cup butter or margarine*
> 3 *tablespoons cocoa*
> 1/2 *tablespoon salt*

Add to mixture:

> 3 *cups Quick Quaker oats*
> 1/2 *cup nuts*
> 1 *teaspoon vanilla*

Drop by spoonfuls onto foil. Leave until fully cooled and firm.

16

International Riding

No doubt about it. There's no better way to wrap yourself in a foreign culture than by bicycle. Just as in America, you'll find that your opportunities for interacting with the "real people" will be increased dramatically. By routing yourself along the rural backroads, you'll be kept at arm's length not only from traffic, but from the plethora of tinsel traps offering everything from plastic Eiffel Towers to Big Ben alarm clocks. Admittedly, this same routing may one day lead you into a confounding corner where no one seems able to "parlez Anglais." But quite often, it's just such situations that can ultimately lead to some of your most unforgettable memories.

One caveat, however, seems in order here. Generally speaking, the only good times that arise from ignorance or confusion are simple problems occurring within the society itself: ordering gasoline instead of wine with dinner or consulting your phrase book for the word written on the rest room door. Humorous times *do not* grow out of mistakes made with passport requirements, currency exchange, or baggage limitations. Unless you have a particular bent to study the inside of consular offices or donate currency to strengthen foreign economies, these are things that you must know before you go. The following advice should get you rolling in the right direction—whatever your direction may be.

RESEARCHING YOUR DESTINATION

Visiting a foreign country by bicycle can be more than a little overwhelming. At first there will be far more around you that seems strange

than is familiar. To avoid feeling like you've just landed on another planet, I highly recommend that you do a little research into the customs of the people and the various kinds of attractions that will await you down those intriguing foreign byways. If you'd like to approach your destination with some good armchair reading, try "Culturgrams." These are basically very concise notes on the customs of various countries throughout the world, produced by Brigham Young University's Center for International and Area Studies. They are extremely inexpensive and can at least get you thinking in the terms of the countries you plan to bicycle. Get the scoop from the Center by writing them at: Box 61-X FOB, Provo, UT 84602 (801-378-6528).

Uncle Sam can provide you with another good way to test the waters of a foreign country long before you leave. The Superintendent of Documents has a great collection of folders called "Background Notes from Countries of the World." They run about $2 each, or you can obtain a collection of all the current notes for the year (usually about 75 or 80) for $34. There is also a subscription available for the same price, which ensures that you will receive all updated notes as they are published throughout the upcoming year. These offer an amazing amount of insight into a country's politics, economics, religions, and customs, and will at least allow you to spark a few interesting conversations with the people you run across during your adventure. Drop the Superintendent of Documents a line at the U.S. Government Printing Office, Washington, D.C. 20402. Alternatively, you can order notes over the phone using Mastercard or Visa by calling the GPO at 202-783-3238.

At last, we come to the more traditional guidebooks. Without belaboring the point, I will say that there are some very good guides, and some that you could have copied out of your sixth grade geography book. For sightseeing in Europe, give the Michelin Green Guides a close look. There is probably nothing more comprehensive on the market today. (It is the Michelin Red Guides that rate the hotels and restaurants.) If you plan to do some walking in any of Europe's more famous cities, try the excellent series entitled *Turn Right at the Fountain,* published by Holt, Rinehart and Winston. For some of the best in budget travel, go with the *Let's Go* series by the Harvard Student Agencies.

As for non-European countries, the Norton/Benn Blue Guides are quite good and can be easily stuffed into a front handlebar bag for quick access. Fodor's, while not quite so compact, will give you a great deal of valuable information you'll need to know before departing, as well as a blurb on the usual hot spots. If Japan or China is your port of call, be sure to check the *Reader's Guide to Periodic Literature* at your local library. Over the past couple of years a great number of magazine articles have been written about visiting these countries, and these may provide some insights not found in most guidebooks. For those on a budget looking to the Middle East, the *Let's Go* series (also commonly available through your library) comes through again.

Additional information can be obtained by writing to the cycling organizations listed in the Appendix, as well as through the consulates and embassies listed in the *World Wide Chamber of Commerce Directory,* as mentioned in Chapter 6.

MAPS

As far as maps go, it all depends upon your destination as to whether you'll be able to pick up maps in the U.S. suitable for actual route planning. If you stay in Europe, the Michelin 1:200,000 and 1:400,000 series will meet most of your needs. (For a list of current offerings, write: Michelin Guides and Maps, P.O. Box 5022, New Hyde Park, NY 11042.)

Bartholomew maps—out of Scotland—are also very good for riding through much of Europe; but like many map companies, Bartholomew has no real distribution in the U.S. Some cyclists simply prefer to make general routing decisions before leaving home and then pick up actual routing maps once they arrive in the destination country. This is sometimes mandatory when visiting some of the lesser-traveled places, such as Africa, Australia, and parts of Asia. If your trip will take you to such faraway places, by all means contact an appropriate cycling organization (see Appendix) well before leaving. Such assistance in route planning can be invaluable.

Regarding scale, you can get by on 1:400,000 maps and save money by purchasing fewer sheets, but if you can possibly afford it, stick with 1:200,000 or 1:250,000 instead. These will cover an area approximately 70 by 110 miles—a good compromise between detail and wide coverage. If you're on a budget, try to purchase 1:400,000 maps for countries that you'll simply be traveling through on your way to somewhere else, and go with the more detailed scale for those areas in which you plan to linger a bit longer.

When you're stuck in a city without a map, you might first check out the phone book. As in the U.S., it will often have a street guide with key landmarks and government offices marked. If you can find on the map the spot you want to get to, point the location out to a passer-by. More often than not, this will result in a wealth of directions. If you don't understand the language, have a pad and pen available with which the person can draw you a map. Sometimes, merely mentioning the name of the town or landmark you want to go to will elicit a response.

PASSPORTS AND VISAS

Passports can be obtained from one of about a dozen offices of the U.S. Passport Agency in major cities or at county courthouses and selected post offices. Come armed with an original or certified copy of your birth certificate, two identical photos of yourself, measuring two inches square on nonglossy paper, and taken in the last six months, and $42 ($27 for children). Your passport will be valid for 10 years. It will usually take from three to six weeks to receive it, though it's possible to have delays during the spring rush.

Another foreign entrance requirement that you may have to deal with is a visa. These are usually stamps that are added to your existing passport and are obtained from embassies, consulate offices, or the United Nations office of the country in question. The process of obtaining a visa can take quite awhile, so plan on doing the paper work long before you hit the road. The simplest do-it-yourself travel technique is to first obtain your passport and then mail it to the appropriate U.S. consulate offices for stamping. You will have to indicate what days you plan on being in the country. Extended stays may require special permits. Many travel agencies have "visa services," which will (for a price) take care of all this stamping and mailing for you. In New York and Washington, D.C., there are services that will hand-deliver your passport to the various United Nations offices or embassies to obtain the proper visas. If your time is limited, or you simply don't care to hassle with such arrangements, these services are well worth the money.

You may want to carry additional passport photographs if you plan to wait to obtain a visa upon entering another country. In a few places the visa is actually a separate document, in which case additional photographs will definitely be required. Also, remember that some countries, such as New Zealand, will require that you enter with a departure ticket already in hand.

All in all, a travel agent is the best person to check with for up-to-date visa requirements. In most African and Asian countries, all visitors need one. In others areas, requirements will be set by the length of stay. Most European countries do not require them at all. Though it's sometimes hard to anticipate, give some serious thought to your potential for prolonged wanderlust before leaving home, and then check into the requirements you'll have to meet to carry it out.

Remember to keep all travel documents *on you*, not in your luggage. Some people use fanny packs or money belts for this purpose. Another way to go is to wrap the documents in plastic, and then fashion a canvas pouch that can be attached to your belt and hung *inside* your pants. This is a very secure way of carrying documents and the plastic bag will guard against rain or perspiration. If you use a wallet, either put it in your front pocket or place it inside of a sock and then wrap a nylon strap around your ankle above the wallet. Front handlebar bags with shoulder straps are also a popular way to go, so long as you don't get so excited with the scenery that you forget them. For added security, use a waist strap with the bag in addition to the one that hangs over your shoulder—much like the setup on many of the better camera bags.

GETTING THERE

Unless you have a good deal of time available, you'll probably elect to fly overseas rather than take a ship. Airlines used to limit free baggage by weight, typically 44 to 66 pounds, depending on the class you travel. Recently, however, there has been a major shift to using *size* as the qualifier and limiting the freebies to two pieces. This is not necessarily good news for bicyclists. Several airlines have made special provisions for two-wheelers, but by all means check on this well before departure. Of course, you can pay extra for oversized luggage, but it could easily cost you $75 to $100 extra on a routine trip to Europe.

There are so many variations and changes made in airline regulations that a list of them would be out-of-date before it hits print. You should by all means check with the carrier as close to your departure date as possible, and perhaps again just before taking off for the airport. Ask for specific luggage size and weight requirements and whether or not there are any special packaging regulations for bicycles.

As for insurance, baggage (including bicycles) and personal possessions can be insured up to $2,000 against loss or damage anywhere in the world. If you plan on having the airline assume responsibility for your luggage disappearing into a black hole en route, you'll have to report it missing within four hours after landing.

If you will be touring with a European, British, or Japanese bicycle in its country of origin, it's not a bad idea to either take your bill of sale with you or register it with U.S. Customs before leaving the country. This will prevent an inspector from trying to charge you duty on it as if it had been purchased abroad.

A final word about flying: "Jet lag" is for real. The best way to avoid it is to get lots of rest before leaving, eat lightly while in the air, and plan easy riding schedules for your first one-to-three days overseas. Climbing on the saddle at the airport and expecting to pedal 75 miles, is usually a big mistake.

ALTERNATIVE FORMS OF TRAVEL

By now, you've probably heard all about the wonders of Eurailpasses. Keep in mind, though, that they are a savings only if you plan to ride the trains fairly often. For two or three train rides, it may be a better deal to simply buy individual tickets. Students of any age and people under 21, for example, can get as much as half off the purchase of single tickets to any of 15 European countries, by contacting "Trans-alpino," 224 Shaftesbury Avenue, London, England, WC2.

If you do decide to go with a Eurailpass, you'll have to buy it from an authorized agent *before* you leave home. Besides first-class travel on 100,000 miles of railroad track, it will gain you passage aboard a number of ferries, lake steamers, buses, and Mediterranean ships operated by the railroad company. If you're under the age of 26, be sure to go with the Eurail Youth Pass, which will give you unlimited second-class travel for about 40 percent less. For more information, write to: Eurailpass, c/o WBA, 51 Ridgefield Avenue, Staten Island, NY 10304.

Although there is seldom any problem with carrying your bike aboard a European train, the methods and charges for doing so will vary from country to country. In some countries the railway employees will load it for you, while in many others you'll have to do it yourself. Sometimes it will be considered a piece of baggage and taken free, but in other cases you should be prepared to spend an additional $2 to $5 for its passage. Also, keep in mind that not all trains carry bikes—only those with baggage cars. To save yourself from the ultimate headache of a lost bike, be sure that your bike will be traveling on the same train as you will. This is an especially important consideration when crossing international borders. Finally, plan to arrive at the station a good 45 minutes before departure whenever you and your bike will be riding the rails together.

There is also an unlimited bus travel program in Europe called "Europabus." This can be used for basic unlimited travel, as with the

Eurailpass, or you can opt for one of their specialized tours. Contact them at 11 East 44th Street, New York, NY 10017. Remember that there are similar rail and bus travel programs that have begun in other countries, such as those in southern Asia. Many of the passes, however, cannot be purchased except in the country for which they are designed. Check with a travel agent for details.

If you don't want to hassle with taking your own bike, you may want to consider renting one instead. This is especially common in Europe and parts of Eastern Asia, where both bike shops and, to a lesser degree, train stations, will have a fair number of two-wheelers up for grabs. *Bicycle Touring in Europe*, by Karen and Gary Hawkins, offers a fairly comprehensive listing of shops and stations that rent bikes across the continent. If you do decide to go this way, just remember that you will probably end up with a lot less bike than you are used to. Though some people do elect to go long distances with rentals, I feel that they are perhaps better for localized touring of a single city or cluster of small towns.

ROUTING

It's a good idea to get in touch with a cycling organization in the country you plan to visit, if for no other reason than to get information on routing (see Appendix). In well-developed countries, your strategy will be to ride the secondary routes, much the same as you would in America. Sometimes, however, these routes can become difficult to find. And certain areas, such as the southern Mediterranean coast, are often dangerous places to ride, with few alternative routes available. If you are determined to see such areas, at least go during the week, or even better, during the slack tourist season. Another option would be to go by bus or train.

In the less-developed countries of Africa, Latin America, and parts of Asia, there is sometimes a different kind of problem. Secondary routes are often dirt or gravel, and can get so dusty with traffic that they become nightmares to ride on. Your only alternative may be to ride on busy primary roads, which rarely have anything that you would recognize as a shoulder. In such cases, you should stay in close touch with local authorities and resign yourself to the fact that your route may at times consist of little better than the lesser of two evils. For the truly adventurous with strong rims and spokes, however, it is unlikely you will ever regret the experience.

PARTS AND MODIFICATIONS

Many cyclists who ride the boondocks elect to go with 26-inch wheels to better withstand the horrible roadways. Be advised that you may have to make modifications to the brakes so that they will reach the rims. This can get expensive, and you should consult your local bike shop about this well before your departure date. Also, though much heavier, puncture-proof tubes are a good idea, especially in the desert areas of Africa and the Middle East, where certain plant thorns litter even the major roadways.

Carry *all* bike parts that you might need. Expect to go through tires much faster than you would in North America. Though, of course, you'll be adding a bit to your weight load, realize that certain parts are simply nonexistent in many regions of the world. Not long ago, a cycling group in Africa was delayed several days while a replacement part for one member's bicycle was flown in from Italy. Needless to say, it was a rather expensive operation. The kind of bikes ridden in most Third World countries bear little resemblance to the wonderful 10-speeds that we tend to take so much for granted. (Remember also that most tools will usually be gauged metrically—*not* in inches.)

As discussed in Chapter 4, a kerosene stove will be your best bet when riding outside of Europe and North America. If you'll be staying in Europe, you can get by with butane, which is sold in many campgrounds throughout the continent.

SPENDING THE NIGHT

Hostels are certainly one of best ways to see the world on a budget. You'll find them to be great for meeting other people, and in many countries they are much more plentiful than in the U.S. Contact the American Youth Hostel before leaving home, to get the latest scoop on membership, foreign guides, and regulations (address in Appendix).

If you're planning on camping in other countries, you should by all means obtain an International Camping Carnet. Many foreign campgrounds are actually owned by clubs, and admittance is often gained only by having this card (which, by the way, will also provide you with any necessary public liability insurance). For more information, write the National Campers and Hikers Association, 7172 Transit Road, Williamsville, NY 14221.

In the more frequently visited parts of Europe and eastern Asia, you may have to adjust your definitions of what you consider to be a crowded campground. During the summer in the more popular areas, they often fill up by late morning—not exactly fitting to the agenda of a typical cyclist. Also, as is true in America, more and more campgrounds in the colder foreign climates are closing up early in the fall. Obtaining camping guides from a national tourist bureau located in America well before leaving home is highly recommended.

Alternatively, in much of the world you can usually receive permission to unroll your sleeping bag on someone's private property. This practice can, in fact, be a great way to gain more contact with the local residents. To ensure your continued welcome, however, do remember to ask first.

Bed and breakfast establishments, now so popular in the United States, have been standard fare in many countries for quite some time. These are fantastic places for meeting people, and the prices are often much lower than in many of the more typical motels. There are now bed and breakfast guides out for much of the world. You would be well-advised to make reservations (where accepted) as early as possible, since these facilities can usually handle only a few people at a time. Your travel agent may be able to provide you a list of bed and breakfast establishments for the countries you're interested in, and in some cases can make reservations for you. This is also the place to check on staying in castles, sometimes plain but rather magical accommodations to be found throughout much of Europe.

Finally, if you've got a destination to travel to by train, consider being rocked to sleep on the rails. In many countries there are what is known as "couchettes," which are really inexpensive versions of the standard sleeping car, complete with blankets and a pillow. They are available for both first- and second-class travelers, and are therefore perfect for both holders of Eurailpasses, as well as Eurail Youth Passes. You'll want to be sure to always make reservations in advance for such accommodations. Compared to the cost of most hotels, couchettes represent a tremendous bargain.

EATING AND DRINKING

As you may have discovered sometime in the past, milk products are not always the cyclist's best friend. In some people milk fats tend to be digested very slowly, which can make the first couple of hours of riding after eating a rather uncomfortable affair. But in many parts of the world, the fats in milk products may be up to two-and-a-half times as concentrated as the levels allowed in the United States. The best strategy is to eat milk, ice cream, cheese, and butter with caution at first, until you've established that they are causing no unusual digestion problems.

It is also not uncommon to find that the different spices in foreign dishes do not sit well with you. People with this problem should consider going with two of the world's most popular staples—beans and rice. If you happen to find them together, you will be getting a complete protein, which will stick with you quite well when riding. The other form of salvation comes from shopping for fresh fruits and vegetables at local markets. In fact, learning the proper word for "market" should be right up at the top of your vocabulary list. Just be sure to wash all fruits and vegetables well before eating. (You can make doubly sure of getting rid of any contaminates by washing the food in a weak tincture of iodine mixture—three drops per quart of water.) Breads are also a safe way to go, and they make for good light lunches or dinners when combined with cheese and fruit.

As for the advice to be careful when drinking the water, I'm afraid that in some parts of the world it is well-founded. Tea and coffee are good alternatives since they have usually been made with boiled water, but you may one day find yourself in a place that serves neither, or what it has has not been boiled to an adequate degree. It's far safer to opt for bottled beverages, which may typically mean beer, wine, bottled fruit juice, or mineral water. In Mexico and Central America, "pulque"—a drink made from the fermented sap of the maguey plant—is a good, slightly alcoholic alternative to water and it's loaded with vitamins and minerals. Although cyclists should avoid drinking alcohol in excess to avoid dehydration, moderate amounts should cause you no problems when combined with plenty of fruits and fruit juices.

All in all, if you simply cannot live without a drink of water, buy mineral or purified water. Should you for any reason decide to drink questionable water, by all means boil it or treat it with a good purifier or both; and don't forget that those creepy little microorganisms are just as potent when taken in the form of ice cubes.

FINANCES

If there is one thing to get a handle on before leaving, it's currency exchange rates. You *do not* always get equal rates of exchange for your American dollars at each place offering the service, nor is it always the same each day of the week. Basically, do all your cashing of traveler's checks at a bank—the larger the better. Many hotels, stores, and restaurants will offer this service, but may charge you for it, and will almost certainly give you a less advantageous rate of exchange. Transacting such business in the middle of the week will probably afford you a better rate than what you will get Friday through Sunday.

One way to avoid getting a bum exchange deal is to buy "destination currency checks," which are essentially travelers' checks issued in the currency of the country you plan to visit. Also, try to have a little foreign cash on hand to take care of any expenses you may encounter upon landing. This can be obtained from a large bank in any major American city.

In many foreign countries, don't expect to be able to lean too heavily on your credit cards. The same movement away from plastic that American service stations have initiated because of outrageous credit company fees is being echoed in hotels and restaurants around the world. But then in some countries, charge fever never caught on in the first place.

As for having money wired to you to rescue you from the depths of financial despair, it is a rather risky proposition. If the money does in fact arrive at all, it will not be for several days—perhaps even a week. All in all, running short in foreign countries can be a rather trying affair.

A FINAL WORD

When riding in your own country, it's often the scenery that plays the most important role in routing your trip. But when you go abroad, the surest way to have a fantastic time is to make your primary consideration *people.* When you're in doubt about something, ask. Stay in campgrounds, hostels, and bed and board establishments once in awhile even if you can afford the best of hotels. There you'll meet travelers from all over the world and engage in conversations that will really germinate the world wanderlust in you. Whenever possible, make a sincere effort to learn some of the language of the people you're visiting. A simple "hello" or "how are you?" can go a long way in establishing a bond of friendship.

Finally, don't fall into the common trap of comparing foreign means of doing things with the "better way" back home. Don't forget, most of the countries you will be visiting have been around much longer than the United States. If you look and listen closely, you'll find bits of wisdom and understanding that profoundly reflect this stability and sense of heritage.

Appendix

Biking Organizations

United States

American Youth Hostels, Inc. (AYH)
1332 I Street NW—8th Floor
Washington, DC 20005

Bikecentennial
P.O. Box 8308
Missoula, MT 59807

League of American Wheelmen (LAW)
10 East Read Street
P.O. Box 988
Baltimore, MD 21203

Foreign

Bicycle Institute of New South Wales
399 Pitt Street
Sydney, New South Wales 2000,
Australia

Canadian Cycling Association
333 River Road
Vanier, Ontario
Canada K1L 8B9

Dansk Cyclist Forbund
Kjeld Langes Gade 14
DK-1367 Copenhagen K Denmark

Cyclist's Touring Club
c/o CTC National Headquarters
Cotterell House
69 Meadow Godalming
Surrey, England GU7 3HS

Touring Club de France
65 Avenue de la Grande-Armée
16 Paris, France

Irish Cycling Federation
287 Castletown
Leixlip County
Kildare, Ireland

Touring Club Italiano
Corso Italia 10
Milan, Italy

Touring Club of Japan
Dainimaejima Building 5F
1-9 Yotsuya, Shinjuku-ku
Tokyo 160, Japan

Todos en Bicicleta
c/o Morales
Pirineos 239
Col Porteles Mexico
13 D.F. Mexico

Gijsbert Valstar
Tidemanstraat 9-c
3022 SB Rotterdam
Holland, Netherlands

Skylistenes Landsforening
Majorstuveien 20
Osla 3, Norway

Pedal Power Foundation of Southern
Africa
P.O. Box 457
Bellville 7530
Republic of South Africa

Scottish Cycling Association
7 Bruntsfield Crescent
Edinburgh 10, Scotland

Touring Club Suisse
Rue Pierre-Fatio 9
1211 Geneva 3, Switzerland

ADAC
Baumgartner Street 53
Munich 70, West Germany

STATE MAPS

State of Alabama Highway Department
Bureau of State Planning (Map Room)
11 South Union Street
Montgomery, AL 36130

Alaska State Chamber of Commerce
310 Second Street
Juneau, AK 99801

Arizona Department of Transportation
Advanced Planning Section
206 South 17th Avenue, Room 310B
Phoenix, AZ 85007

Arkansas State Highway Department
Map Sales, Room 203
P.O. Box 2261
Little Rock, AR 72203

California Department of Transportation
P.O. Box 1499
Sacramento, CA 95807

Colorado Department of Highways
Room 117
4201 East Arkansas
Denver, CO 80222

Connecticut Department of
Transportation
24 Wolcott Hill Road
P.O. Drawer A
Westerfield, CT 06109

Delaware Department of Transportation
Highway Administration Center
P.O. Box 778
Dover, DE 19901

District of Columbia Department
of Transportation
Room 519 Presidential Building
415 12th Street NW
Washington, D.C. 20004

Florida Department of Transportation
Maps and Publications, Mail Station 12
605 Suwannee Street
Tallahassee, FL 32301

Georgia Department of Transportation
Room 10, 2 Capitol Square
Atlanta, GA 30334

Hawaii Department of Transportation
Planning Branch
600 Kapiolani Boulevard
Honolulu, HI 96813

Idaho Transportation Department
P.O. Box 7129
Boise, ID 83703

Illinois Department of Transportation
Map Sales
2300 Dirksen Parkway, Room 217
Springfield, IL 62764

Indiana State Highway Commission
Room 1101 State Office Building
100 North Senate Avenue
Indianapolis, IN 46204

Iowa Department of Transportation
Transportation Information
800 Lincoln Way
Ames, IA 50010

Kansas Department of Transportation
Chief of Transportation Planning
State Office Building, 8th Floor
Topeka, KS 66612

Kentucky Department of Transportation
Map Sales
419 Ann Street
Frankfort, KY 40622

Louisiana Department of Transportation
and Development
P.O. Box 44245
Baton Rouge, LA 70804

Maine Department of Transportation
State Office Building
Augusta, ME 04330

Maryland State Highway Administration
Map Distribution Office
2323 West Joppa Road
Brooklandville, MD 21022

Massachusetts Bureau of Transportation
Planning and Development
Department of Public Works
150 Causeway Street, Room 301
Boston, MA 02114

Michigan Department of Transportation
Bureau of Transportation Planning
P.O. Box 30050
Lansing, MI 48909

Minnesota Department of Transportation
John Ireland Boulevard, Room B-20
St. Paul, MN 55155

Mississippi Transportation Planning
Division
P.O. Box 1850
Jackson, MS 39205

Missouri Highway and Transportation
Department
Public Information Division
P.O. Box 270
Jefferson City, MO 65102

Montana State Department of Highways
Montana Travel Promotion Unit
Helena, MT 59601

Nebraska Department of Roads
Information Office
Box 94759
Lincoln, NB 68509

Nevada Chamber of Commerce
Association
P.O. Box 2806
Reno, NV 89505

New Hampshire Department of Public
Works and Highways
John O. Morton Building
85 Loudon Road
Concord, NH 03301

New Jersey State Chamber
of Commerce
Five Commerce Street
Newark, NJ 01702

New Mexico State Highway
Department
1120 Cerrillos Road
P.O. Box 1149
Santa Fe, NM 87503

New York State Department of
Transportation
Map Information Unit
Building 4, Room 105 State Campus
Albany, NY 12232

North Carolina Department of
Transportation
P.O. Box 25201
Raleigh, NC 27611

North Dakota Tourism Promotion
Capitol Grounds
Bismarck, ND 58505

Ohio Department of Transportation
Map Sales, Room B-100
P.O. Box 899
Columbus, OH 43216

Oklahoma Department of
    Transportation
Reproduction Branch
200 NE 21st Street
Oklahoma City, OK 73105

Oregon Department of Transportation
Travel Information Section
101 Transportation Building
Salem, OR 97310

Pennsylvania Department of
    Transportation
Publication Sales
P.O. Box 134
Middletown, PA 17057

Rhode Island Department of
    Transportation
Public Information Office
State Office Building
Providence, RI 02903

South Carolina Department of
    Highways and Public
    Transportation
P.O. Box 191
Columbia, SC 29202

South Dakota Division of Tourism
221 South Central
Pierre, SD 57501

Tennessee Department of Transportation
James K. Polk Building, Suite 15
Nashville, TN 37219

Texas Department of Transportation
P.O. Box 5064
Austin, TX 78763

Utah Department of Transportation
Planning Division
4501 South 2700 West
Salt Lake City, UT 84119

Vermont Agency of Development and
    Community Affairs
Travel Division
61 Elm Street
Montpelier, VT 05602

Virginia Department of Highways and
    Transportation
Map Office
1221 East Broad Street
Richmond, VA 23219

Washington State Department of
    Transportation
Public Affairs Office
Highway Administration Building
Olympia, WA 98504

West Virginia Department of Highways
Public Information Division, Room 1052
1900 Washington Street East
Charleston, WV 25305

Wisconsin Department of Transportation
Map and Document Sales
P.O. Box 7713
Madison, WI 53707

Wyoming Highway Department
Planning and Administration
P.O. Box 1708
Cheyenne, WY 82001

(The above agencies can also assist you
with country road map information, or
direct you to the appropriate source.)

CANADIAN MAPS

Travel Alberta
Alberta Tourism and Small Business
    Association
14th Floor, Capitol Square
10065 Jasper Avenue
Edmonton, Alberta T5J 0H4

British Columbia Ministry of Tourism
1117 Wharf Street
Victoria, British Columbia V8W 2Z2

Travel Manitoba
Department 2069, Legislative Building
Winnipeg, Manitoba R3C 0V8

New Brunswick Department of Tourism
Promotion Branch
P.O. Box 12345
Fredericton, New Brunswick E3B 5C3

Newfoundland Tourist Services Division
P.O. Box 2016
St. John's, Newfoundland A1C 5R8

Travel Arctic
Government of the Northwest
    Territories
Yellowknife, Northwest Territories
    X1A 2L9

Nova Scotia Tourist Information Centre
P.O. Box 130
Halifax, Nova Scotia B3J 2M7

Ontario Travel
Queen's Park
Toronto, Ontario M7A 2E5

Prince Edward Island Services Division
P.O. Box 940
Charlottetown, Prince Edward Island
    C1A 7M5

Gouvernement du Quebec
Ministere de L'Industrie, du Commerce
    et du Tourisme
Case Postale 20,000
Quebec, Quebec G1K 7X2

SaskTravel
Saskatchewan Tourism and Renewable
    Resources
3211 Albert Street
Regina, Saskatchewan S4S 5W6

Tourism Yukon, Government of Yukon
Box 2703
Whitehorse, Yukon Territory Y1A 2C6

Topo Maps

Areas WEST of the Mississippi River:
U.S. Geological Survey
Box 25286
Federal Center
Denver, CO 80225

Areas EAST of the Mississippi River:
U.S. Geological Survey
1200 South Eads Street
Arlington, VA 22202

Maps of Major Cities

Rand McNally and Company
Customer Service Department
Publishing Group
P.O. Box 7600
Chicago, IL 60680

NATIONAL FOREST MAPS

DEPARTMENT OF AGRICULTURE
REGION, REGIONAL FORESTER, ADDRESS, AND TELEPHONE

Missoula, MT 59807:
  Charles T. Coston
  Federal Bldg., 406–329–3011

Lakewood, CO 80225:
  Craig W. Rupp
  11177 W. 8th Ave., 303–234–3711

Albuquerque, NM 87102:
  M. Jean Hassell
  517 Gold Ave. S.W., 505–766–2401

Ogden, UT 84401:
  Jeff M. Sirmon
  324 25th St., 801–626–3011

Milwaukee, WI 53203:
  Steve Yurich
  633 W. Wisconsin Ave., 414–291–3693

Atlanta, GA 30367:
  Lawrence M. Whitfield
  1720 Peachtree Rd. N.W.,
    404–881–4177

Portland, OR 97208:
  R. E. Worthington
  319 S.W. Pine St., 503–221–3625

San Francisco, CA 94111:
  Zane G. Smith, Jr.
  630 Sansome St., 415–556–4310

Juneau, AK 99802:
  John A. Sandor
  Federal Office Bldg., 907–586–7263

Recommended Reading

Bike Touring: The Sierra Club Guide to Outings on Wheels, by Raymond Bridge, Sierra Club, 1979. This covers many of the traditional touring subjects, including clothing, loading techniques, and camping gear. The book is particularly valuable for its discussions of various bicycle components.

Everybody's Book of Bicycle Riding, by Thom Lieb, Rodale Press, 1981. This book covers a wide variety of general cycling subjects on a basic level. Topics include bicycle setup, riding techniques, commuting, and some good on-the-road advice. There's one significant thing about Lieb—he knows what he's talking about.

Glenn's Complete Bicycle Manual, by Clarence W. Coles and Harold T. Glenn, Crown, 1973. This is the manual to use for repairing everything from coaster brakes to 10-speeds. Its particular strength is the excellent black and white photographs and line drawings—the clearest to be found anywhere. A great companion for the would-be mechanic.

The Bicycle Touring Book, by Tim and Glenda Wilhelm, Rodale Press, 1980. A big, fat book of touring basics, covering everything from finding a touring partner to riding with a loaded bike. A great place to begin.

Index

Other Mountaineers books you'll enjoy:

BICYCLING THE BACKROADS AROUND PUGET SOUND
Erin and Bill Woods' guide to 54 recreational bicycling routes in the
Puget Sound basin, from Olympia to the San Juans, from Port Or-
chard to the Cascades. Details, maps, elevation profiles.

BICYCLING THE BACKROADS OF NORTHWEST OREGON
Philip N. Jones guides the cyclist to 40 trips, ranging from Portland
south to Eugene. Routes vary in length from 10 miles to nearly 150.
Details, maps, elevation profiles.

BICYCLING THE PACIFIC COAST
Tom Kirkendall and Vicky Spring give complete details, maps,
photos, elevation profiles and sidetrips for the 1,947.3-mile route between Mexico and Canada.

MILES FROM NOWHERE
Barbara Savage's delightful narrative of a two-year, 23,000-mile,
25-country bicycle tour around the world. ". . . an entrancing tale."—
Library Journal. ". . . jammed with adventure, humor, pain, exhaustion. . ."—San Diego Union. ". . . the most delightful travel literature I
have ever read."—Santa Barbara News-Press. ". . . a life-affirming
book."—Women's Sports

Write for illustrated catalog of over 100 outdoor titles

The Mountaineers • Books
306 2nd Avenue W., Seattle, WA 98119